Margaret Ellin Cromer

Books by M. F. Sweetser.

ARTIST BIOGRAPHIES. *New Edition.* Illustrated. 7 vols., 16mo, cloth, $8.75; half calf, gilt top, $17.50; half polished morocco, $17.50. Sold in sets only.

VOL.
  I. Raphael and Leonardo.
 II. Angelo and Titian.
III. Claude Lorraine and Reynolds.
IV. Turner and Landseer.
 V. Dürer and Rembrandt.
VI. Van Dyck and Angelico.
VII. Murillo and Allston.

NEW ENGLAND. A Guide to the Chief Cities and Popular Resorts of New England, and to its Scenery and Historic Attractions. With six maps and eleven plans. $1.50.

THE WHITE MOUNTAINS. A Guide to the Peaks, Passes, and Ravines of the White Mountains of New Hampshire. With six maps and six panoramas, including the new Appalachian Club Map. $1.50.

THE MARITIME PROVINCES. A Guide to the Chief Cities, Coasts, and Islands of the Maritime Provinces of Canada. With four maps and four plans. $1.50.

HOUGHTON, MIFFLIN AND COMPANY.

BOSTON AND NEW YORK.

ARTIST BIOGRAPHIES

IN SEVEN VOLUMES
VOLUME VII

ARTIST BIOGRAPHIES

MURILLO

ALLSTON

BOSTON AND NEW YORK
HOUGHTON, MIFFLIN AND COMPANY
The Riverside Press, Cambridge

Copyright, 1877 and 1878,
By JAMES R. OSGOOD & CO. AND
HOUGHTON, OSGOOD & CO.

ILLUSTRATIONS.

MURILLO.

The Immaculate Conception	*Frontispiece*
Portrait of Murillo	66
The Infant Christ twisting a Crown of Thorns	88
The Spanish Flower-Girl	106
The Assumption of the Virgin	118

WASHINGTON ALLSTON.

Portrait of S. T. Coleridge	74
Portrait of Washington Allston	134
The Witch of Endor	174

MURILLO

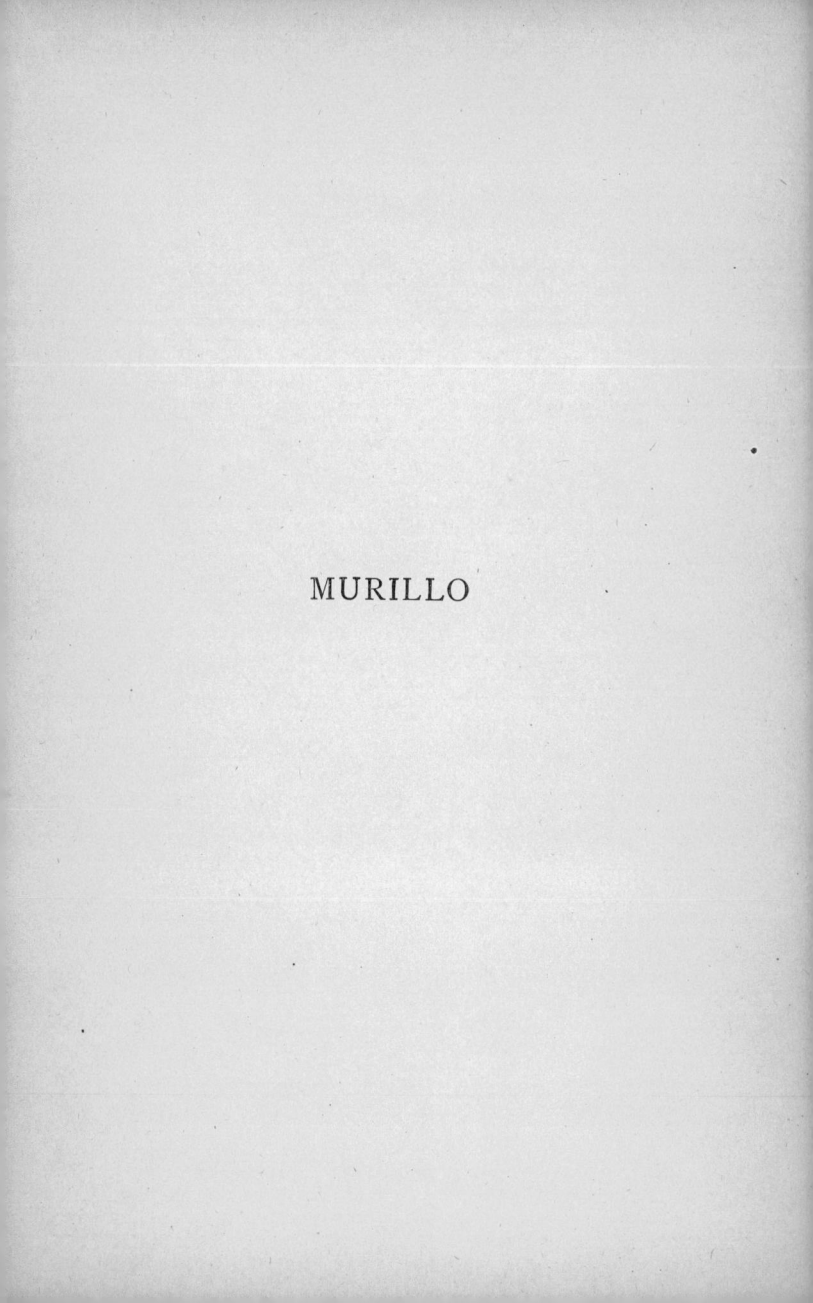

PREFACE.

THE biographer of Murillo is confronted at the outset with a serious difficulty arising from the great lack of reliable and available material on the subject of the great artist's life. His career was so uneventful and of such simple elements, that it has been neglected by Spanish writers, as well as the careful British scholars, by whom the whole world is ransacked for themes worthy of study. The German critics also, although they have closely scanned and deeply theorized over the mediæval art of Italy and Northern Europe, have paused before the sealed gates of Spain, and remained silent.

The present work is the first memoir of Murillo published in America, and probably the only one in the English language, if we except a small and soon-forgotten sketch issued in London many years since, containing a meagre paraphrase of Cean Bermudez. I have sought earnestly "beside all waters," to secure fresh accounts of this most interesting artist, and to

PREFACE.

gather more ample details as to his private and home life. These efforts have met with some measure of success; but still we find (to use the hackneyed phrase of artists' biographers) that the life of the man is shown forth in his works, and that their description best exemplifies his character.

The following books were consulted in the preparation of this biography: Cean Bermudez's "Diccionario Storico de los mas Illustres Professores de las Bellas Artes en España" (vol. ii.); Stirling's "Annals of Artists in Spain;" Sir Edmund Head's "Handbook of the French and Spanish Schools;" Stothert's "French and Spanish Painters;" and Scott's "Murillo and the Spanish School;" also, under careful reserve, the works of Blanc, Viardot, Quilliet, and Cumberland. Information has been gleaned from the travels of Gautier, Teste, Chasles, Andersen, Hare, Rose, Poitou, Lady Tenison, Baxley, Thornbury, Roberts, Inglis, Lady Herbert, Mrs. Ramsay, Baxter, Urquhart, Mrs. Tollemache, the guide-books of Ford and O'Shea; and the hand-books to Seville, written by Varflora and Standish.

M. F. SWEETSER.

CONTENTS.

CHAPTER I.
1617–1645.

Birth of Murillo. — Not Priest, but Painter. — Castillo's Studio. — Market-place Pictures. — Van Dyck's Disciple. — Journey to Madrid. — Studies. — Velazquez 7

CHAPTER II.
1645–1655.

Seville's Greatness. — Sudden Popularity of Murillo. — His Marriage. — The *Cálido* Style. — "St. Anthony." — The *Vaporoso* Manner 22

CHAPTER III.
1655–1658.

The Immaculate Conception. — History of the Dogma. — The Rules of the Inquisition as to Paintings. — The Solemnity of Spanish Art 44

CHAPTER IV.
1658–1670.

The Academy of Art. — Rival Painters. — Murillo's Slave. — Invitation to Madrid declined. — The Master's Home and Circumstances. — His Children. — His Disposition 55

CHAPTER V.
1670–1674.

Murillo's Great Paintings at La Caridad. — Don Miguel Mañara. — "Moses Striking the Rock." — "The Loaves and Fishes." — El Tiñoso 68

CHAPTER VI.
1674–1676.

Capuchin Pictures. — Trouble with Iriarte. — "The Children of the Shell." — "St. Ildefonso." — "St. Bernard's Vision" . . 79

CHAPTER VII.
1676–1682.

The Nun-Daughter. — The Old Priests' Pictures. — Augustine Illustrated. — Murillo's Sickness. — His Will. — His Death . . 92

CHAPTER VIII.
1682–1693.

Murillo's Style. — His Madonnas. — *Genre*-Painting. — The Beggar-Pictures. — Portraits. — Landscapes. — Limitations . . . 101

CHAPTER IX.

Spanish Art and Seclusion. — Soult. — Collections of Murillo's Works. — Drawings. — Murillo and Velazquez. — Later Artists of Spain 112

MURILLO.

CHAPTER I.

Birth of Murillo. — Not Priest, but Painter. — Castillo's Studio. — Market-place Pictures. — Van Dyck's Disciple. — Journey to Madrid. — Studies. — Velazquez.

BARTOLOMÉ ESTEVAN MURILLO, the last and greatest of the illustrious painters of mediæval Spain, was born in the city of Seville, late in the year 1617, and was baptized on New Year's Day, 1618, in the Church of La Magdalena. His parents were Gaspar Estevan and Maria Perez; and the name of his maternal grandmother, Elvira Murillo, was added to his own, according to an Andalusian custom. Cumberland says that the family had once been opulent and distinguished, and was still highly respectable; but it does not appear to have been in even moderate pecuniary circumstances.

The child was at an early day consecrated to the service of the Church; and his parents fondly hoped that in due time they should see him in the robes of a priest. But it was not long before they found that his genius led him in another direction, where, indeed, he could serve God in a nobler manner.

An early tradition of his life tells how one day Maria Perez went to church, leaving him at home; and when she returned she found that the child had transformed the household picture of Jesus and the lamb into an irreverent caricature. He had replaced the glory around the Infant Saviour's head by a portrayal of his own hat, and had metamorphosed the lamb into a dog. Usually the torments of the Inquisition would have racked the perpetrator of such a sacrilege; but in this case probably the tender years and innocent unconsciousness of the offender pleaded sufficiently for his pardon.

During his school-days, the lad was more given to making rude sketches on his books than to studying their contents; and marked the budding of a precocious genius by scrawling pictures on all convenient walls and other plane surfaces.

His education at this time was not prolonged beyond the acquisition of the simple rudiments of reading and writing; for his parents marked his artistic gropings, and determined to have him taught in the profession toward which he showed such an instinctive adaptation.

At an early age, therefore, Murillo was placed in the studio of his maternal uncle, Juan de Castillo, to learn the principles of art. Castillo was then about fifty years old, and was one of the leaders of the school of Seville, including among his pupils not only his young nephew, but also the afterwards famous Alonso Cano and Pedro de Moya. He had been a student under Luis Fernandez, from whom he had acquired the prevalent Florentine traditions of the sixteenth century, combining chaste designing with cold and hard coloring. It was well that young Murillo was thus early grounded in purity of conception and dignity of arrangement; for the contemporary development of an indigenous Spanish art came in good time to help him to the elements lacking to complete success.

Seville was in those days one of the great world-centres of art, related to Spain as Florence had been to Italy, or as Antwerp afterwards was to the Low Countries. The three chief schools were presided over by Castillo and his two former fellow-students in the studio of Luis Fernandez; Herrera the Elder, whose style was powerful and violent, and his temper not less so; and Pacheco, the Inquisition's art-critic, who had taught Velazquez and Cano. Another school was formed by the disciples of the Canon Roelas, who had won high fame as a painter of Jesuits. Between the pupils of these masters a warm emulation was kept up, which was further stimulated by hopes of the favor of the wealthy clergy and nobles, or by a yearning for the applause of the citizens.

The students gave much time to the preparation of *bodegones*, or small pictures portraying eatables, fruit, game, and utensils. In this way practice in the use of colors was easily carried on, with familiar objects as models; and the resulting pictures were readily sold to the tavern-keepers of Andalusia. In his earlier days the great Velazquez himself was famous for the accuracy and verisimilitude of his *bodegones*.

Even in these years of immaturity, the youth showed the amiability and industry which ever characterized his disposition; and these traits soon endeared him to his master and his fellow-students. Castillo was very careful in his instruction, and taught him the nature of the pigments, and how to grind them, and to prepare the canvas, and manipulate the palette and brushes. The costly appliances of modern institutes of art were not available in the Sevillian studios; and the schools of design were domiciled at the dwellings of the masters, whose household expenses were defrayed from the common fund of the students. The models for practice were limited to a few sketches, or certain casts and bits of antique sculpture, with a rude lay-figure on which various draperies were hung. Living models were rarely used; and the frugal students avoided such heavy expenses by posing to each other in turn, showing such members as were to be copied by their comrades.

When he was about twenty years old, and still in Castillo's studio, Murillo painted two Madonnas, in the cold and formal style of his teacher One of these showed Our Lady with St. Francis and a monk, and was executed for the Convent of Regina Angelorum; the other contained the Madonna and St. Dominick, and was hung in the College of St. Thomas. A few other cold pictures of this rudimental time are preserved in Seville, rather from historic interest than on account of their intrinsic merit, which is small.

The scene of these early labors was a house in the Calle de las Tiendas, in his native parish of La Magdalena. The church of this parish, in which he was baptized, was destroyed by Soult's French troops in 1810.

By working steadily and intelligently, and losing no opportunity to improve himself, Murillo advanced surely and rapidly, and equalled his master in a few years. About the year 1640 Castillo removed to Cadiz, leaving his pupil at once without an instructor, and in an unsatisfactory position towards the world. His parents were probably dead, for they are heard of no more; and the young man was left with empty pockets, to shift for himself. Evidently he could not join the pupils of the illustrious Zurbaran, much as he might wish it; for it now became necessary for him to labor for his daily bread. He was therefore driven to the *Feria*.

The weekly market of the *Feria* was held in

front of the Church of All Saints, and was visited not only by hundreds of rustics, gypsies, monks, and citizens, but also by dozens of street-artists. These shifty Bohemians found their studios in the open air, and often worked with such speed that a picture was finished while its price was being discussed. Such hasty and ill-considered work was of course inferior, insomuch that the phrase *una pintura de Feria*, as applied to a picture, was the reverse of flattering. The merest tyros in the use of colors, without theoretical instruction or regulated practice in drawing, acquired in this rough school a certain fearless mechanical facility and off-hand dexterity, which subsequent study expanded into respectable talent. One of their ancient annalists says that they always carried their brushes and colors to the market-place, with which, at the suggestion of a customer, they could in a few minutes transform a bristling St. Onophrius into a St. Christopher, or a Madonna into a St. Anthony of Padua, or even into a representation of the souls in Purgatory. Great numbers of these rude pictures were bought by the colonial merchants, and shipped to Mexico and South America, with accompanying saints' bones and plenary indulgences, wherewith the churches of New Spain were highly edified.

For about two years Murillo worked in this strange manner, standing among the rude merchandise of the market, and peddling out for trifling sums pictures which are now almost priceless. Yet even this humble work was valuable in its final results, for it tended to give him freedom of touch and manual dexterity. Still his designing was feeble, and his coloring poor and cold, if we may judge by a Madonna of that period now in the Seville Museum.

Some writers claim that Murillo visited America during his youth; but no mention of such a journey was made by his contemporaries and friends, and later biographers discredit the statement. Probably it originated from the fact that large invoices of his paintings were sent to the New World about this time.

Other writers, mostly Italians, state that he made an excursion to Florence and Venice, to study the masterpieces of Tuscan and Titianesque art. But an equal silence as to this alleged voyage is found among his friends, and modern chroniclers decline to accept the theory of the Italian journey. He had intended to go to Rome in 1642, to study the great works of art there preserved, but concluded that he could learn quite as much at Madrid. For many years it has been agreed that Spain's foremost painter never went beyond the borders of his own country.

Early in the year 1642, Murillo met with a powerful assistance in the person of his former companion Moya, who had grown weary at the restraints of Castillo's studio some years before, and entered the army. The Spanish infantry was then campaigning in Flanders; and as he followed the flag through the rich old Lowland cities, and saw the wonderful works of the Flemish painters, he felt a new interest in art. The manner which most impressed him was that of Van Dyck; and he journeyed to London, and became a disciple of that illustrious master. Right well and earnestly he must have worked; for when Van Dyck died, six months later, Moya returned to Seville impregnated with the Flemish ideas, which he imparted to his old comrade.

Moved by Moya's romancing stories of foreign travel, adventure, and study, Murillo determined to go abroad himself, and see what he also might learn, — whether in art-cradling Italy, or among the enterprising souls of Northern Europe. Poor he was indeed, but his profession should pay his way. He bought a great quantity of canvas, which he cut into small squares, primed and prepared these alone in some garret of Seville, and then covered them with rude paintings of merchantable subjects. Among these crude daubs were church-banners, Madonnas, bleeding hearts, saints, flower-pieces, and landscapes, which were sold in the mass to a speculative ship-owner. They were sent to America and the West Indies, and sold to the pious colonists of Spain in the New World.

Thus equipped with funds, Murillo departed from Seville secretly, without apprising even his nearest friends (his parents were dead). But, instead of shipping from one of the adjacent ports for Naples or Antwerp, he went northward on foot across the Sierras to Madrid, a long and harassing journey at the best of times. At last the ambitious youth of twenty-five entered the capital of Spain, friendless and poor, but fearless and indomitable. It seems that his intention was to go to Rome, for he sought introductory letters there. The illustrious Velazquez, a native of Seville, was at this time at the summit of his fame, and held the office of painter to the King. To him Murillo went on his arrival, to seek advice, and letters to the Roman artists. The old master had a long interview with him, in which much was said of fair Seville, the tenets of Castillo, the family of Murillo, and his motives in making a journey into Italy. Velazquez was pleased with the manner and the ideas of his young townsman, and took him to dwell in his own house, making liberal offers for his immediate advantage.

The young man's desire to see and study excellent pictures and Italian masterpieces was readily satisfied by his new friend, who procured him admission to the Escurial, the Buen Retiro, and the other royal galleries. The Madrid collections were then rich in fine pictures of the older Italian schools, as well as of the later Flemings and the contemporary native artists; and a new wonder-land was here opened to the painter of the market-place.

During Murillo's sojourn at Madrid, it is

intimated that his position under the patronage of Velazquez enabled him to have favorable intercourse with the artists then in Madrid. Among these were Mayno, the Dominican, who had been taught by Titian's pupil Domenico delle Grecche; Leonardo, who adorned the Buen Retiro Palace; Zurbaran, "the Spanish Caravaggio," one of the loftiest names in Iberian art; Caxes, whose father was a native of Italian Arezzo; Ariás, the painter of the royal portraits; Pereda, who worked in the Buen Retiro; Collantes, the landscape-painter; and Roman, the pupil of Carducho and Velazquez. Alonso Cano, who has been called "the Spanish Correggio," was also in Madrid at this time, having fled from Andalusia after wounding Valdes in a duel. He killed his wife not long afterwards, and yet was honored with a canonry in the Cathedral of Granada.

Doubtless Murillo also met many of the prominent artists of the provinces, when they came up to the capital from time to time. Among the most prominent of these were Martinez and Horfelin of Saragossa, Espinosa of Valencia, Toledo and Moya of Granada, Saavedra of Cordova, and Herrera el Mozo and Pacheco of Seville.

STUDIES AT MADRID.

The latter, whose official duty it was to preserve the pious orthodoxy of Spanish art, was a frequent visitor at the house of Velazquez, who had married his daughter Juana.

Murillo spent nearly three years in Madrid, a period which was devoted to the closest study of the masterpieces in the public galleries, under the advice of Velazquez. Many of these he copied with great care, as if to penetrate the secrets of the masters by treading closely in their footprints; and Titian, Rubens, and Van Dyck were constantly contemplated by him in many of their richest works. Much time he also gave to drawing and modelling, both from living figures and statuary, so that the warm Venetian and Flemish coloring which he was acquiring should be happily aided by correct designing.

Murillo had been at Madrid but a few weeks when he was deprived of the guidance of Velazquez, who attended his royal master in a journey to Saragossa. The unwise measures of the Prime Minister Olivarez had forced both Portugal and Catalonia into insurrection; and the King went across the northern Sierras to overawe the latter province with his presence. The court did not return to Madrid until late in the autumn; and in the meantime the young painter diligently devoted himself to copying the masterpieces of Van Dyck, Ribera, and Velazquez. When his patron returned from the seat of war, he was astonished and delighted at the student's success, and recommended him to concentrate his attention still further on the works of these three artists. He also showed his copies to the King, and placed Murillo on friendly terms with the Prime Minister and other *virtuosi* of the court.

During much of the years 1643 and 1644, Velazquez was absent with the King, in the northern war. In 1643 Olivarez was deposed from the royal ministry, and banished to an obscure hamlet of Leon, where he died of a broken heart. Murillo was deeply pained by the downfall of the friendly Premier; and perhaps his disgust with Madrid dated from that event. When the court returned from the victorious siege of Lerida, early in the autumn of 1644, Velazquez was so much pleased by his protégé's new works, that he advised him to visit Italy immediately, and offered him letters of introduction to eminent Roman and Tuscan artists, with aid in other directions from the King himself.

But the young artist had already decided against going abroad, and determined to return home, despite the urgent counsel of his patron. Probably he concluded that he had now studied enough, and had mastered the secrets of Italian art as thoroughly as he could have done in sight of the Apennines. Perhaps, also, there were family reasons compelling his return; for when he went to Madrid he had left his sister in care of her uncles, and doubtless had some responsibility about her future. Early in 1645, therefore, he returned to his native city.

CHAPTER II.

Seville's Greatness. — Sudden Popularity of Murillo. — His Marriage. — The *Cálido* Style. — "St. Anthony." — The *Vaporoso* Manner.

AFTER his settlement in Seville, Murillo entered upon a long and unbroken season of incessant labor, making pictorial reproductions of many varying subjects with rapid and skilful hand. The greater part of his existing works date from this period, and show a remarkable evenness in strength and coloring. A considerable number of pictures issued from his studio between 1645 and 1650, in the first of his three manners. Viardot maintains that he remained in Seville from 1645 until his death; but there is reason to suppose that he visited Cadiz at least once after his return from Madrid.

Nearly all of Murillo's life was passed in that terrible period of Spain's decline, the reign of Philip IV. "Misrule at home, oppression, rapacity, and revolt in the foreign provinces, bloody and fruitless wars, declining commerce, defeat and disaster in all quarters of the globe, and at last an inglorious peace, — these are the events which mark the forty-four years' reign of Philip IV. . . . While province after province raised the standard of rebellion, and his superb empire was crumbling to dust, the King of the Spains and the Indies acted farces in his private theatre, lounged in the studios, sate in solemn state in his balcony at bull-fights or *autos-da-fé*, or retired to his cabinet at the Pardo, to toy with mistresses, or devise improvements in his gardens and galleries."

In the Low Countries, Rembrandt, Douw, and Teniers were at work; in Italy, Guido, Domenichino, and Carlo Dolce; in France, Claude and Poussin: but scant tidings of these illustrious masters reached Andalusia. In England, Cromwell subverted the monarchy, and founded the Commonwealth; on the Continent the *Grand Monarque* destroyed the cities of the Rhine, and broke up the Triple Alliance; and from the Everglades of Florida to Massachusetts Bay and ice-bound Newfoundland, bands of intrepid adventurers were founding a vast new Christian realm.

Yet how little did these momentous events change the even tenor of life in the Guadalquivir valley! Not even the summons of his King could call Murillo from his tranquil studio by the Moorish wall, to exchange the altars and the sunshine of his dear Seville for the splendors of the capital.

What, then, was the princely city, from whose walls no temptation could lure its gifted son? Founded by the Phœnicians, aggrandized by the Romans, capitalized by the Goths and Vandals, enriched by the Moors during their sojourn of five centuries, and held as capital of Spain until Charles V.'s reign,— it was one of the most splendid cities of Europe, and one of the chief marts of the New-World trade. The vast and grandiose cathedral was finished a century before Murillo's birth, with its solemn twilight of stately aisles, and its overflowing wealth of matchless Gothic tracery. By its side stood La Giralda, richer in history and legend than any campanile of Giotto or of St. Mark, jewelled with Saracenic ornaments, and lifting its lace-like stone-work 340 feet into the blue sky. A few rods distant was the royal palace of the Alcazar, built and adorned by Moslem architects to rival the Alhambra, and filled with the best workmanship of Granada. The ponderous Lonja, or Exchange, was near at hand, and in its grand simplicity showed the genius of the architect of the Escurial, while in its long galleries the archives of the New World were stored. Time fails us to speak of the mysterious and pre-historic Golden Tower of Cæsar; of the hundred and sixty towers on the old Saracenic walls; of the orange-laden parks by the bright Guadalquivir; of the picturesque Moorish houses, rising in every street; of the hundred and forty churches and converted mosques, whence incense was ever rising to the Immaculate Virgin.

The surrounding territory was the Tartessus of the Phœnician geographers, Tarshish of the Hebrews, Bætica of the Romans, and Vandalusia (Land of the Vandals) or Andalosh (Land of the West) of the Saracens. It is the garden of the peninsula, the Hesperia, rich in golden orange-groves and prolific corn-fields, with a genial and equable climate the year round. The people were the descendants of the Latinized Punic Iberians, enriched with Gothic blood, Moslems for half a millennium, and then Mary-worshippers for four centuries, — decadent, unwarlike, marvellous braggarts, but volatile and sparkling, light-hearted and friendly, abhorring work, and seeking pleasure, not always in the narrow paths of rectitude.

Seville is not only the city of Astarte and Figaro, but has the prouder honor that within its territories the illustrious Trajan was born, and also Theodosius the Great, and other chiefs of the Roman Empire. After literature had become extinct at Rome, smothered by the riotous excesses and unspeakable sensualism of the degenerate citizens, Seneca and Lucan, natives of Andalusia, revived the glories of Latin culture on the banks of the Guadalquivir.

In Murillo's day it was the richest city in the Spanish dominions, and the most beautiful after Lisbon and Naples. Fleets of vessels frequently ascended the Guadalquivir, heavily freighted with the products of the Americas, and gladly faring homeward to "the glory of the Spanish realms." The ecclesiastics of the city held many learned and eloquent men among their number, including Rioja the poet, Caro the antiquary, and Roa the hagiologist. In the stately semi-oriental palaces along the bright plazas, the noble descendants of ancient houses dreamed away the charmed hours, and calmly enjoyed the beauties of "La Terra della Santisima." Their chief was the valiant Duke of Alcalá, the Mæcenas of Andalusia, who was himself both soldier, and scholar, and painter. His palace contained a famous art-gallery and library, and was the home of the culture of Seville.

The old renown still clings to the fair capital of Andalusia; and Byron's praise of " Seville, famous for oranges and women," is echoed in Poitou's words of yesterday: "The Spaniards boast of Seville as the pearl of their cities, and the Spaniards are not wrong." The ancient Iberian proverb is still current: —

> "He who Seville has not seen
>   Has not seen a marvel great;
> Who to Granada has not been
>   Can have nothing to relate."

The first works executed by Murillo after his return from Madrid were a series of paintings in the Convent of San Francisco, in which connoisseurs discern reminiscences of Van Dyck, Velazquez, and Ribera. The Franciscans had a noble convent near the Casa del Ayuntamiento, with three hundred marble columns in its cloisters; and they resolved to appropriate for the decoration of its minor cloister a sum of money which one of their most able mendicants had collected. With a thrift which closely approached parsimony, they offered so small a compensation for this work, that the masters of the Sevillian schools of art disdained to notice them. But Murillo, needy and friendless as he was in his own city, seized the offer as an opportunity for displaying his prowess, and forthwith immortalized the convent-walls by illuminating them with the light of his genius.

For the next three years, most of the artist's time was devoted to the execution of eleven paintings for the Franciscan cloisters. The first of these represented St. Francis, resting on his iron bed, and listening in devout ecstasy to the melodious notes of a violin which an angel is playing to him. The noble conception of this work is filled out with a Riberesque strength of coloring and an original tenderness of tone.

The second picture portrayed St. Diego of Alcalá, asking a blessing on a kettle of broth, which he is about to give to a group of beggars at the gate of his convent. The cluster of ragged pensioners is depicted with rare fidelity and force, and illustrates one of the artist's favorite themes of study.

The names of the third and fourth subjects have not been preserved, though Bermudez says that they contained several fine heads. The fourth was distinguished by the singular accessory of a globe of fire, in which the soul of Philip II. ascends to heaven.

The finest picture of the series is that representing the death of St. Clara of Assisi, who was consecrated as a nun by St. Francis himself. She is shown in the rapturous trance in which her soul passed away, surrounded by pale nuns and emaciated monks, and looking upward to a splendid contrasting group of Christ and the Madonna, with a train of celestial virgins bearing her shining robe of immortality.

The companion-picture for the St. Clara contains a Franciscan monk, who passes into a celestial ecstasy when cooking in his convent-kitchen, and is kneeling in the air, while angels perform his culinary tasks. This was executed in 1646.

The seventh, eighth, and ninth subjects are

now forgotten. The tenth picture showed St. Giles, the Athenian prince who wandered to a hermitage in Languedoc, and became the patron of all forests and of Edinburgh town. He is delineated in ecstasy before Pope Gregory IX., and four other figures appear in the background.

Another picture of this series contains a Franciscan monk praying over the body of a dead brother friar, as if to restore it to life. This work is now owned by Mr. Richard Ford, of Heavitree, Devonshire, and was the only one not removed from the convent by the French.

The pictures in the Franciscan cloister remained the pride of Seville for 170 years, until the irruption of Napoleon's armies into Spain. On the retreat of the French troops, Marshal Soult carried these and many other works of art beyond the Pyrenees, and they were afterwards dispersed through Northern Europe. It was an act of brigandage, but was nevertheless fortunate in its results, for the convent was destroyed by fire soon afterwards.

The quiet and studious youth who had left his obscure home three years before, to visit Madrid, was almost unknown in the city; but when he was seen to have returned with such rich acquisitions, he was universally acknowledged as the head of the Sevillian school. The chief families of the city vied in their attentions to the rising genius, and aided him to make a high social position for himself. Orders for portraits flowed in from all sides; and monks and ecclesiastics strove together for his altar-pieces. Artists and critics crowded the Franciscan cloister to study the new works, and acknowledged that Herrera and Zurbaran were fairly surpassed by this phenomenal painter, who vied with and equalled at will Ribera, or Velazquez, or Van Dyck. Pacheco, indeed, seems to have been jealous of the new-comer, not on his own account, for his own inferiority was too evident, but even for the supremacy of his son-in-law Velazquez; and so he refrained from mentioning Murillo in his work on art.

The paintings of the next three years mark the first of the three periods of his art life, when he was in transition from a palpable eclecticism to a distinct and original manner. During this stage his outlines were hard, and his lights and shadows were contrasted almost as strongly as those of Caravaggio. Now and then there appears a marked trait of Titian or Rubens, Zurbaran or Van Dyck, showing that the fruits of the imitative studies at Madrid had not yet been thoroughly assimilated. This first manner was called by Spanish critics the cold (*frio*) style, in distinction from the warm (*cálido*) style which followed it.

His humble imitation of his great predecessors in art was not of long duration, and the subsequent eclecticism also soon passed away. Murillo's personality was too strong, and his individuality too intense, to allow him to become a contented follower; and in due time he dropped every reminiscence of the Titianesque and the Flemish, and developed his own independent and inimitable style.

The most popular portrait of Murillo is the one now in the Louvre, which he painted of himself about the year 1648, and retained until his death, when it passed to his sons. It affects to be drawn on a stone slab, which rests on another similar slab, whereon the master's name is inscribed. This portrait has been engraved several times, and was copied by Sir David Wilkie. It shows a strong and pleasing face, with firm lips, and a high brow rising over keen and intelligent eyes.

By the year 1648 Murillo appears to have become wealthy and of high renown; for at that time he married a lady of distinguished family, Doña Beatriz de Cabrera y Sotomayor, who possessed a considerable property, and dwelt at the village of Pilas, a few leagues south-west of Seville. The popular tradition is that he first saw her while painting an altar-piece in the Church of San Geronimo, at Pilas, and won her love while portraying her as an angel in that picture. Her married life appears to have been as domestic and uneventful as that of Titian's wife Cecilia; for no details of it have been preserved, and she is not known to us even in a portrait. The subsequent management of Murillo's household seems to have been both faithful and wise.

Several of the master's Madonnas have features so much resembling each other, and so evidently portraits, that they were probably drawn from the same model, whereof the painter wished to preserve the outlines of the face with perfect faithfulness. It has been conjectured that these idealized likenesses were drawn from the countenance of the wife of Murillo.

Three children were the result of the marriage, — Gabriel, who went to America; Francisca, afterwards a nun; and Gaspar, the future canon of Seville Cathedral. Several of the master's beautiful pictures of the infants Jesus and St. John were painted with one of his boys for a model.

The new establishment of Murillo, graciously presided over by the high-born Doña Beatriz, became the resort of the best society of Seville, and was famous for its hospitable re-unions of the local artists. A social position, which the best triumphs of his pencil could have won but slowly, was insured to him by his fortunate matrimonial alliance.

Soon after his marriage, the master abandoned his first manner in painting, and assumed a warmer and more original style. The outlines were less sharp and pronounced, and the figures were fuller and rounder, with deep atmospheric effects and tender and luminous coloring. The reminiscences of other great artists, which so often appeared in his works between 1645 and 1659, are no more seen afterwards; and no academic formalism remains to impair the realistic power of his designs. Flemish and Italian traditions cease to affect him; and the sacred personages portrayed are all Andalusian, not only in lineaments, but even in expression and sentiment. In the close imitation of visible truth he surpassed all the *naturalistas* of the local schools; and his execution is marked by a rare simplicity and suavity. The works of the new manner are notable for graceful and well-arranged drapery, skilfully disposed lights, harmonious tints, soft contours, and a portrait-like naturalness in the faces, lacking in idealism, but usually pure and pleasing. His flesh tints were almost uniformly heightened by dark-gray backgrounds, and were so amazingly true that one of his critics has said that they seemed to have been painted with blood and milk (*con sangre y leche*).

This was the so-called warm (*cálido*) manner, which was preserved, according to some accounts, for twenty years. It appears, however, that although the *vaporoso* style was developed later in the master's practice, he never abandoned the *cálido* entirely, but retained it in combination with the other, thus making powerful contrasts in his pictures.

The earliest work in this second manner was an Immaculate Conception, which the Brotherhood of the True Cross placed in the Franciscan Convent. It was finished in 1652, and the artist received 2,500 reals, or $125. When Murillo painted this theme, for the cupola of the Franciscan Church, he threw great vigor and *chic* into the work, since it was to be viewed only from a distance. But the prominence of these traits, and the absence of delicate finishing, displeased the monks when the picture was deposited in their convent-hall; and they refused to accept such a rude daub. Murillo craved the favor of being allowed to place it in the dome before he took it away; and when the brethren saw the marvellous effect which the masculine power of the picture produced when at its proper focal distance, they repented them of their fault-finding, and desired to retain it. But the artist punished them for their blind criticism by exacting double the original price of the picture. A similar story is told of Phidias and the Athenians, and another of Van Dyck and the canons of Courtrai.

THE SAINT-ARCHBISHOPS.

In 1654 Francisco Pacheco died, at the ripe old age of eighty-three, during which time he had done much to elevate the art of Spain, chiefly by his writings and instruction. After his death, Murillo appears to have become the head of the Andalusian painters, and gathered around himself the literary and artistic circle which formerly frequented Pacheco's studio.

In 1655 Don Juan Federigui, the archdeacon of Carmona, commissioned the master to portray the two Murcian brothers, Sts. Leander and Isidore, who were archbishops of Seville in the sixth and seventh centuries, and fought the Arian heresy. They are represented in mitres and white robes, enthroned in the archiepiscopal seats; but are both too short for absolute symmetry. St. Leander, the Apostle of the Goths, bears the mild and venerable features of Alonso de Herrera, the marker of the cathedral-choir, with an expression of dignity, gentleness, and sagacity. St. Isidore — *Egregius Doctor Hispaniæ* — is younger in appearance, vigorous and intellectual, but stern and uncompromising, like the busy and fearless controversialist that he was. These pictures are now in the sacristy of the

Cathedral of Seville, of which city the two saints are the patrons and guardians.

"The Nativity of the Virgin" was painted at about the same time, for the high altar of the Seville Cathedral, and was one of the best composed and most pleasing of the master's works. It shows a group of women and angels dressing the new-born Mary, with Sts. Anne and Joachim beyond, in front of a sunny landscape, while the warm upper air is traversed by exultant cherubs. The bare and rounded left arm of one of the maidens was the envy of the Sevillian ladies, and would have sorely troubled the prudish Pacheco, could he have lived to see it.

The Cathedral clergy seem to have been well pleased with the works of their painter; for in the following year they ordered a large picture of St. Anthony of Padua, for which they paid 10,000 reals. Herein appears the kneeling saint, with rapturous eyes and outstretched arms, regarding the apparition of the Infant Jesus, who is descending in a flood of glory, surrounded by a company of graceful and innocent cherub-children. On the massive table beside the saint is a vase of white lilies, concerning which many persons averred, even before the artist's death, that they had seen birds fly down the cathedral-aisles, and peck at the flowers. To those who might cavil that if St. Anthony had been painted as well as the lilies, the birds would have been afraid to approach, the simple answer was ready, that in Spain monks and birds get on very well together.

This famous picture was repainted in 1833, and lost much of its original beauty. One of the canons told M. Viardot that the Duke of Wellington offered to pay for it as many gold pieces as would cover its surface of fifteen feet square, — a sum of about $240,000. This improbable story was also repeated to Widdrington, and is still current in Seville. In 1874 the picture was stolen from the Cathedral, and nothing was heard of it for some time; until two men offered to sell it for $250 to Mr. Schaus, the picture-dealer, at New York. He purchased the work, and turned it over to the Spanish consul; and not long afterwards the Sevillians received back the gem of their Cathedral with great joy.

It was after studying this composition and those in the Franciscan cloister, that Antonio

Castillo y Saavedra, the nephew of Murillo's first master, and a pupil of Zurbaran, cried out in surprise: "It is all over with Castillo! Is it possible that Murillo, that servile imitator of my uncle, can be the author of all this grace and beauty of coloring?"

During the same year, the canon Don Justino Neve y Yevenes, one of Murillo's warmest friends, commissioned him to paint four large semicircular pictures for the adornment of the renovated church of Santa Maria la Blanca, a beautiful little structure, which had formerly been a Jewish synagogue. The two which were hung in the nave illustrated the fourth-century legend of Our Lady of the Snow, wherein it is said that the Blessed Virgin appeared by night to a pious Roman senator and his wife, commanding them to build a church in her honor on the Esquiline Hill, on a spot which they should find covered with snow. The next morning they went to the Esquiline, attended by a great company of priests and people, and found a snow-bank glittering there in the August sun; and on this site they erected the sacred basilica, which was afterwards replaced by the superb Church of Santa Maria

Maggiore. Murillo's first picture shows the noble senator, in the black velvet costume of a Spanish grandee, soundly sleeping in his chair over a great book, with his wife also reposing on the floor by his side, to whom appears a lovely Madonna, seated on a cloud in the midst of a brilliant glory. In the second picture, they are telling their dream to the stately old Pope Liberius; and in the background the procession is seen nearing the miraculous snow on the Esquiline. The other two pictures represented a group of saints adoring Our Lady of the Immaculate Conception, and another blessed company kneeling before a figure of Faith, holding the Eucharistic elements. The same church also contained Murillo's pictures of the Mater Dolorosa, St. John the Evangelist, and the Last Supper; all of which, except the last (one of his earlier works), were carried away by the French armies. The two representations of Our Lady of the Snow were returned after the fall of Napoleon, and are now preserved in the Academy of San Fernando, at Madrid.

The last of the three manners of Murillo was the *vaporoso*, or misty, with soft and tender outlines, velvety coloring, and shadows which are only softened lights. Herrera el Mozo had introduced this style of painting into Andalusia, where it became very popular. It has also been suggested that the master adopted this vague and indeterminate manner because it obviated the necessity of careful finishing, and thus enabled him to execute more pictures with less work. A similar charge has been made against Turner. But Viardot dissents from the general opinion that Murillo's *frio*, *cálido*, and *vaporoso* manners followed each other in the order of time and development; maintaining that he used them all at the same time, adapting the style to the theme, — the *frio* for his beggars and gypsies, the *cálido* for the saints, and the *vaporoso* for the Immaculate Conceptions and Assumptions.

In the first of the pictures executed for Santa Maria la Blanca, the master developed this third or vapory style, in which he afterwards executed such noble works. In this manner the rigidity of the outlines of his first style is altogether abandoned, and they fade away naturally into the light and shade. There is a feathery lightness of touch apparent, as if the brush swept over the

THE MISTY MANNER.

canvas smoothly, and with unbroken evenness; and this saintly softness is enhanced by frequent contrasts with harder and heavier mundane groups in the same picture. The refined tenderness and delicacy of the new manner constitute the chief peculiarities by which the great Sevillian is now known, and are combined with a careful and winning adherence to nature. The formal and academic are avoided in all these later works, in favor of simplicity and earnestness.

CHAPTER III.

The Immaculate Conception. — History of the Dogma. — The Rules of the Inquisition as to Paintings. — The Solemnity of Spanish Art.

THE Mystery of the Immaculate Conception was Murillo's favorite subject; and the rare sentiment and poetic grace of his representations of the theme have won for him the title of "The Painter of the Conception." In the very year of his birth, Pope Paul V. issued a bull forbidding attacks on the doctrine of the Immaculate Conception, the dearest dogma of the Church in Spain. "On the publication of this bull, Seville flew into a fury of religious joy. Archbishop de Castro performed a magnificent service in the Cathedral, and, amidst the thunder of the organs and the choir, the roar of all the artillery on the walls and river, and the clangor of all the bells in all the churches, swore to maintain and defend the peculiar tenet of his see. Don Melchor de Alcazar, doubtless the early friend of Velazquez at court, gave a splendid entertainment at the bull-ring, at which his fellow-nobles displayed their liveries and gallantry, and he himself and his dwarf, attended by four gigantic negroes, performed prodigies of dexterity and valor."

The dogma of the Immaculate Conception arose in the fifth century, and was one of the chief points at issue in the mediæval Church. It was held as essential to the honor of the Incarnation, that the Virgin Mother should have been always free from all taint of original sin, either by special exemption before the embryo was formed or her soul entered it, or else by divine sanctification purifying her before she was born. Sts. Bernard and Thomas Aquinas, with the Dominican brotherhood, disputed the radical view of the Conception; but Duns Scotus and the Franciscans upheld it, and were supported by the University of Paris and the Council of Basel. The Council of Trent spoke ambiguously on the subject; and the contest was thereafter waged hotly, until Paul V. forbade disputation on either side, being under the influence of the Spanish Crown. For the next two centuries the doctrine gained ground steadily, and in 1854

Pius IX., after receiving opinions "all but absolutely unanimous" in its favor from the bishops and people of the Church General, declared it to be an article of Catholic belief. In the *Flos Sanctorum*, Villegas admits that the doctrine had but slight foundation in the early Church, but maintains that this apparent omission was divinely ordered, since, if it had been fully known in those unenlightened days, the ancient Christians would have worshipped the Virgin as a goddess.

A consideration of Murillo's pictures, and others of the Spanish school, should be prefaced by a study of the rules to which they were made to conform. The Inquisition, which regulated even the most trivial events of domestic life, exercised a close scrutiny over the domain of Spanish art, and at last deputed Francisco Pacheco, brother of one of its familiars, to "point out to Christian painters the method which they ought to pursue." In the year of Murillo's birth, the Holy Office issued a mandate to Pacheco, saying: "We give him commission and charge him henceforward that he take particular care to inspect and visit the paintings of sacred subjects

PACHECO'S CROTCHETS. 47

which may stand in shops or public places." Thirty years later, in 1648, he published a treatise on the art of painting, telling how pictures should be designed, and what heretic errors must be avoided. The work bore the title of "*El Arte de Pintura, su Antiquedad y Grandeza,*" and was published at Seville.

He attacks Michael Angelo's "Last Judgment" on the ground of the indecency of portraying angels without wings, and saints without clothes; and objects to the scientific absurdity of allowing the damned to float in the air, "when it is matter of faith that they must want the free gifts of glory, and cannot therefore possess the requisite lightness and agility." He reprobates the idea of painting angels with beards, and also that of showing the angel of the Annunciation as flying down with uncovered legs, when he should be all clothed and kneeling before the Madonna. Again he says, "What can be more foreign from the respect which we owe to the purity of Our Lady the Virgin, than to paint her sitting down, with one of her knees placed over the other, and often with her sacred feet uncovered and naked? (Let thanks be given to the Holy Inquisition, which commands that this liberty should be corrected.)" Even in the domestic scenes, when her feet must needs be seen, they should be covered with shoes, since her custom of wearing them is proved by "the much-venerated relic of one of them from her divine feet in the Cathedral of Burgos."

Pacheco says further, of the Immaculate Conception: "But in this gracefullest of mysteries, Our Lady is to be painted in the flower of her age, from twelve to thirteen years old, with sweet grave eyes, a nose and mouth of the most perfect form, rosy cheeks, and the finest streaming hair of golden hue; in a word, with all the beauty that a human pencil can express." But Murillo often contravened these and the subsequent rules by painting dark-haired and sun-browned Virgins, sometimes mature women, with the horns of the moon on which they stand pointing upward instead of the orthodox downward curve, and omitting the regulated crown of twelve stars and the cord of St. Francis. The crescent signifies Isis, Diana, and Mahomet, over whom the Queen of Heaven is at last triumphant, as well as an allusion to the twelfth chapter of Revelation; and the blue and white robe commemorates her ap-

73 - Firenze - Galleria Pitti - Madonna con bambino - Murillo

pearance in that guise to the holy Portuguese nun, Doña Beatriz de Silva.

Minute rules are laid down for the portrayal of the Virgin in each event of her life, with explanations of their reasons and necessity, and other quaint scholastic details. The history of the Annunciation lilies is unfolded with pious prolixity and evident enthusiasm. Pacheco goes on to stigmatize the favorite subject of St. Anna teaching the Virgin; saying, "There can be no doubt that the glory and perfection of the Virgin must have been too great for her to need the teaching of mere created beings, for . . . God accumulated in her all the privileges which he had diffused among all his creatures: from the first instant of her most pure conception she possessed perfect use of reason, free-will, and contemplation; she saw the divine essence; science, natural and supernatural, was poured into her more abundantly than it was granted to Adam or to Solomon."

Further objection is made to the representation of the Infant Christ as naked in His mother's arms, since it is evident that St. Joseph was too well off in the world not to be able to clothe the child. The peculiar form of Christ's sufferings under the crown of thorns is marked out, and supported by the revelation to St. Bridget.

He reviews the fertile subject of dispute as to whether the Saviour was fastened to the cross with three nails or four, and assails the adherents of the former number as partakers in the heresy of the Albigenses; quoting Bellarmine, Rioja, St. Bridget, and the stigmata of St. Francis, as supporting the orthodoxy of four nails.

Artists are forbidden to study living nude figures, and this advice is given: "I would paint the faces and hands from nature, with the requisite beauty and variety, after women of good character; in which, in my opinion, there is no danger. With regard to the other parts, I would avail myself of good pictures, engravings, drawings, models, ancient and modern statues, and the excellent designs of Albert Dürer: so that I might choose what was most graceful and best composed without running into danger." Poor Dürer and the ancients! to what Tartarean realms had they been consigned for Spain's advantage!

An artist of Cordova was punished for depicting Our Lady with a hooped petticoat, and St. John with pantaloons; and Don Luis Pasqual was reprimanded for painting her in a Venetian petticoat with wide round sleeves. A terrible warning was given in the fate of an artist who once made a lewd picture, and when he died passed to Purgatory, being saved from the severer torments of Hell only by the prayers of the saints whom he had portrayed. His unhappy spirit at last persuaded the owner of the evil picture to destroy it by fire; and, when that was done, the painter escaped from Purgatory. A bishop who once celebrated mass before the picture of the Last Judgment, in a Sevillian convent, said that he would rather face a hurricane in the Gulf of Bermuda than officiate again before that fleshly painting.

The danger of too suggestive pictures, and the penalties visited on undevout artists, thus set forth in countless stories, are balanced by many miracles and marks of divine favor extended toward more pious limners. One of these is narrated by Pacheco about an artist who was painting a picture of the Madonna, of which he had finished the face and one arm, when suddenly the platform on which he was working, at a great height, gave way. He cried out, "Holy Virgin, hold me up!" when the painted arm thrust itself forward, and sustained him in mid-air until aid came, when it relapsed again into the wall. Why could not such miracle have befallen our noble Sevillian at Cadiz?

Murillo disregarded the formulæ of the Jesuits as to these paintings, and carried out his designs as best pleased him, producing scores of Madonna-pictures for the churches and convents of southern Spain. Though not strictly orthodox, according to Pacheco's rules, the marvellous beauty of these works aroused the admiration of all the religious communities, and insured for their author the potent favor of the Church.

The short-lived and clearly distinct art of Spain was the subservient handmaid of the Church and the Catholic nobility, led forward on the narrow and ascetic lines of Iberian thought, and appalled away from even a thought of intellectual independence by the sight of the flaming sword of the Inquisition. Image-worship had always been a prominent feature of the Spanish Church, since the fourth century, when the decree of her Council of Illiberis, forbidding the introduction of statues in Christian buildings, was overthrown by the people, not yet converted from the ideas of the Olympian mythology. Thousands of workmen were engaged in carving and painting the images of the saints; and the Second Command passed into desuetude. Statues of saints that could weep, wink, speak, and bleed, were commonly found throughout the peninsula, as they are even to this day, whereby " the Church has been much enriched, and innumerable souls converted." Their memories were carried by the knights of the conquest, even into the terrific solitudes of the New World; and St. Rosa of Lima was soon evolved to guard the land of the Incas with spiritual battalions, and Mexico was electrified by the many miracles of Our Lady of Guadaloupe. The men-at-arms of Coronado bore her sacred banner across the the deserts of northern Texas and even into the heart of Kansas.

The inspired ecstasies and lofty melancholy depicted by the Spanish painters were the outgrowths of their own devout and austere lives. The freedom and laxity in morals of their Italian brethren were unknown in the solemn studios of Spain; nor were their easels occupied simultaneously by Venus and Danaë, the Ecce Homo and the Mater Dolorosa. Luis de Vargas, the founder of the Sevillian school, was constantly at the confessional and the altar, and humbled himself daily by scourging and by wearing hair-cloth shirts. Vicente Joanes, who adorned Valencia, and has eighteen pictures in the Madrid Museum, always prepared himself for painting by confession and communion. Diaz was a familiar of the Inquisition; Mayno was a Dominican; Argensola, a mendicant monk; Martinez, a Carthusian; Cespedes, a prebend of Cordova; Roelas, a prebend of Olivarez; Cano, a canon of Granada; and Leonardo, a monk of Valencia.

Akin to these were the ancient English artists, whom Arundel, the Archbishop of Canterbury, commanded thus: "Whan that an ymage maker shall kerve, caste in moulde, or peynte ony images, he shall go to a prieste, and shryve him as clene as if he sholde than dye, and take penaunce, and make some certeyn vow of fastyng, or of praiynge, or of pilgrimage-doinge, praiyng the prieste specially to praye for hym, that he may have grace to make a faire and devoute ymage."

CHAPTER IV.

The Academy of Art. — Rival Painters. — Murillo's Slave. — Invitation to Madrid declined. — The Master's Home and Circumstances. — His Children. — His Disposition.

In 1658 Murillo began to labor in behalf of his favorite project of founding an academy of art in Seville; and won over his would-be rivals, Valdés Leal and the younger Herrera, to aid in the new scheme. The artists of Madrid had for years been trying to accomplish a similar object, but were unsuccessful, even though backed by the royal influence and interest. On New Year's Day, 1660, the first class of the academy was begun, in a hall of the Exchange of Seville, being composed of students who had already attained some proficiency in art, since elementary instruction was not to be given there. The pupils were required to profess their orthodoxy in the words, "Praised be the most Holy Sacrament, and the pure Conception of Our Lady;" and to practise it by abstinence from profanity, light speaking, or other improprieties. The studies were made mostly from nude forms and lay figures; and colors were used to an unusual extent. Students were freely admitted, on the payment of such a fee as they could afford.

Ten days after the school opened, a society was formed by twenty-three of the leading artists of Andalusia, to direct the studies, govern and advise the students, and mark the grade of the graduates. The necessary expenses of the school were borne by a monthly subscription of six reals from each of these artists, forming a fund which was administered by a major-domo. Their first officers were Murillo, Herrera el Mozo, Llanos y Valdés, Palencia, Schut, and Valdés Leal. Dissensions soon arose among the academicians, and a formidable secession threatened at one time to ruin the society; but within ten years it had become an assured success.

Murillo was the head of the Academy during its first two years, and the founder of its constitution. Afterwards he was less connected with it, whether because it could then go very well alone, or his studio demanded all his time, or he disdained to remain and combat his jealous rivals.

His main design in establishing the school was probably to provide a means whereby young artists could escape the privations of his early life; and also to have the traditions of the masters worthily preserved and inculcated. The Academy nevertheless failed to elevate the art of southern Spain, or even to arrest its rapid decay; and produced only new relays of struggling second-rate painters, drilled into precision and mediocrity.

Later in the year 1660, Herrera deserted from the Academy, and removed to Madrid, where he remained until his death, twenty-five years later. He had studied at Rome, and attained a certain manual dexterity, but was jealous of Murillo, and went away probably to avoid the constant contemplation of his own inferiority.

Valdés Leal was another haughty and consequential artist, who was continually aggravated by his fellow-painter's superiority. Still the two rivals seem to have been measurably intimate, and the story is preserved of Valdés Leal inviting the master to criticise a new picture which he had painted, wherein a rotting corpse was the most prominent feature. Murillo's comment on the work was at once flattering as to its execution, and disapproving as to the design: "*Compadre*, it is a picture which cannot be looked at without holding one's nose."

Pedro de Medina Valbuena was one of Murillo's most intimate friends and associates, and he became President of the Academy in 1667. He secured some valuable contracts for the master, and enjoyed his warm esteem. The banners for the royal fleets on the American coasts were painted by Valbuena, who was skilful in the use of water-colors.

Our artist's mulatto slave, Sebastian Gomez, was assigned to the task of grinding colors, and the menial offices of the studio, but devoted his spare hours to the secret study of drawing and coloring. One day, when the studio was empty, he finished a head of the Virgin, which was sketched on the master's easel; and the astonished Murillo exclaimed, on discovering its author, "I am indeed fortunate, Sebastian; for I have created not only pictures, but a painter." He promoted Gomez to nobler work, and several of his pictures are still preserved and prized at Seville. They are full of rich and tender coloring, and are lacking only in composition.

During the great festivals at Seville, on the canonization of St. Ferdinand, in 1668, a superb memorial volume was published by the cathedral-chapter, treating of Seville and its illustrious men, and of the recent celebrations. Herein, where the master himself could read and enjoy it, Don Fernando de Torre Farfan pronounced a truly Spanish panegyric on the universal renown and the learned pencil of Murillo, "a better Titian," and asserts that Apelles might have been proud to be called "The Grecian Murillo." Furthermore, he said of the picture of "The Immaculate Conception," "that those who did not know that it had been painted by the great artist of Seville, would suppose that it had its birth in heaven."

In 1668 the Cathedral clergy once more devolved a large task on Murillo, employing him to retouch the allegorical compositions of Cespedes, in the chapter-house, and to make eight oval half-length pictures of saints, with a larger Madonna. The latter was a stately and black-haired Andalusian woman, somewhat idealized, and surrounded by garland-bearing cherubs. The saint-pictures included Sts. Justa and Rufina, the fourth-century martyrs, patronesses of Seville, and of the beautiful Giralda tower; St. Hermengild, the Gothic prince and martyr, who was put to death by the Arians; the Archbishops Pius and Laureano; Sts. Leander and Isidore; and King Ferdinand. These pictures are not equal to the master's best work, but are pleasing in character, and well adapted to the use for which they were intended. They are still preserved in the Cathedral.

About the same time the master engaged in the decoration of the Antigua Chapel, for which he painted the Infants Christ and St. John, and the Repose of the Virgin in Egypt. These have all disappeared, and were probably carried to France when Soult gave way before Wellesley's British battalions.

In 1670, or somewhat later, a picture of the Immaculate Conception, by Murillo, was exhibited at Madrid during the festival of Corpus Christi, and awakened great popular enthusiasm. King Charles II. sent to the artist to invite him to enter the royal service; but he thanked the envoy, his good friend Don Francisco Eminente, and begged to be excused on account of his old age. This pretext is at once seen to be unsatisfactory; and the real motive of the master's reluctance was generally supposed to have been to avoid compromising his tranquillity and love of retirement. Perhaps, also, he had some unpleasant memories of Madrid and its fickle courtiers, and of the mournful fate of his patron Olivarez. The invitation may have come from the art-loving Don John of Austria, or the Queen-mother; for the King was but nine years old in 1670. Or a later date may be assigned to the correspondence, when the King was old enough to appreciate, and when the artist's plea might have appeared more reasonable.

Eminente desired at least to take back one of Murillo's pictures to place in the Royal Gallery, but could not wait for a new one. He bought from Juan del Castillo the "St. John in the Desert," for $125, and returned with it to Madrid. It is said that Philip IV. had already commissioned the artist to paint several large pictures of scenes in the lives of the saints, which he sent to Rome as a present to the Pope. The Italian artists and amateurs were greatly astonished at sight of these superb productions of the despised Iberian art, and hailed their author as a second Paul Veronese.

At some time in these latter years, the master painted a new portrait of himself, at the request of his children. This was probably the same which was included in the Aguado Gallery, and has been engraved several times. Herein the great artist has a careworn expression, as if life was not all play, even in Seville. Another portrait of three-quarters length showed him with a cheerier expression, holding a drawing in one hand and a crayon in the other. This appears to have been a repetition and enlargement of the picture in the Louvre, and is now known only by indifferent Spanish prints.

During the latter part of Murillo's life, he dwelt in a large and beautiful house near the Church of Santa Cruz, and not far from the Moorish wall of the city. This honored fabric is still carefully preserved, and is frequently visited by foreign travellers. The court-yard contains a marble fountain, amidst flowering shrubs, and is surrounded on three sides by an arcade upheld by marble pillars. At the rear is a pretty garden, shaded by cypress and citron trees, and terminated by a wall whereon are the remains of ancient frescos which have been attributed to the master himself. The studio is on the upper floor, and overlooks the Moorish battlements, commanding a beautiful view to the eastward, over orange groves and rich cornlands, out to the gray highlands about Alcalá.

Certain recent English travellers have visited and described another house in the same vicinity, on the Plaza de Alfaro, as the home of Murillo; stating that he was accustomed to paint in the garden of the larger one. This second house is small and unpretending, with narrow rooms and a weedy garden. Both these are in the Juderia, or Jews' Quarter, a quiet and retired part of the city. Possibly they were each occupied by the master at different times, the larger one in later years, when he had attained a high social and professional rank. It is clearly established that he died in the large house; and an inscription to that effect was placed there during the present century by its owner and occupant, Don Cepero, the Dean of Seville, who was one of Murillo's most ardent admirers, and saved many of his works from destruction.

There is every reason to suppose that the master enjoyed a comfortable competence during his later years, and kept up a worthy home-establishment. It is true that he received but a few hundred dollars each for his greatest works; but even such sums were princely in that age and country, and would go as far as thousands would now. The proud independence which enabled him to decline a royal invitation to court was not nurtured in a hovel. His sister had married one of the foremost men of Spain; and his children were all richly provided for.

An English collector has a fine portrait by Murillo, depicting a beautiful auburn-haired woman, arrayed in a loose white robe. This has been called the painter's mistress, on no better ground than conjecture, — "a title," says Stirling, "which has perhaps often been bestowed on a very vestal, in order to lend a romantic interest to a picture."

Murillo's sister Teresa made a fortunate marriage, her husband being a noble of Burgos, Don Joseph de Veitia Linage, a knight of Santiago, judge of the royal colonial court, and a lover of art and literature. In 1672 he published at Seville a valuable work on the West Indies; and afterwards was summoned to Madrid, where he became the chief secretary of state, in the year of Murillo's death. Some time previous, he obtained a benefice at Carmona, for the artist's son Gaspar, then a mere schoolboy, which was subsequently changed to a canonry at Seville. Gaspar also became a passable painter, imitating the style of his illustrious father.

Gabriel, the master's elder son, was provided with a rich benefice, worth 3,000 ducats, by the parental influence; and afterwards went to America, where he was living when his father died. Nothing more is known of his history; and even conjecture is silent.

The most prominent trait of Murillo's character was his uniform sweetness of spirit, — a rare trait in southern Spain, if not among great artists generally. It has been suggested that he imitated the noble nature of his fellow-townsman and brother-artist, Velazquez, as well as his admirable style of painting; for there are many points of resemblance between the dispositions of these two heads of Spanish art. They were equally free from the prevalent national foibles of vain-glory and boasting, and possessed remarkable powers of attracting and influencing their fellow-men. Murillo's moderation and tact were conspicuously displayed in the tumultuous early history of the Seville Academy.

The traditions of Seville, as gathered by Cean Bermudez ere they had grown old, represent the management of Murillo's school of art as of a praiseworthy character, contrasting strongly with that of the passionate Herrera. The master was very gentle and painstaking in his care of the scholars, and maintained a paternal and generous friendship for them after they had left the studio. In later years they mourned his death as if they had indeed lost a father.

He became one of the most pious of men, after the manner of Spanish Catholics, and spent hours daily in prayer. He was amiable and gentle in his disposition, yet subject to occasional quick fits of passion and gusty impulses, as was natural to the oriental blood of Andalusia. There is no shadow resting on his fair fame; and his personal life was altogether unobjectionable. His diligence never failed, and his determination to excel did not falter; and through his splendid powers of application he was enabled to lay a broad foundation for the rising fabric of his genius.

VERA EFFIGIES BARTHOLOMÆI STEPHANI A MURILLO MAXIMI PICTORIS
HISPALIENATI ANNO 1613 OBIIT ANNO 1682 TERTIA DIE MENSIS APRILIS.

During his later years the lifelong piety of Murillo became even more pronounced; and he was accustomed to remain in the church often from mid-day until twilight, lost in devout reveries, and forgetting the outer world and its toiling activities. He had always been eminent for his charities and liberal bounty to the poor; and when he died, all the money which he possessed was seventy crowns. He lived as he painted, between saints and beggars, and transferred the riches which he received on account of the one to the aid and uplifting of the other. The inscription on his tomb was the key-note of his life, — "Live as one who is about to die."

CHAPTER V.

Murillo's Great Paintings at La Caridad. — Don Miguel Mañara. — "Moses Striking the Rock." — "The Loaves and Fishes." — El Tiñoso.

The glorious career of Murillo culminated between 1670 and 1674, in his great works for La Caridad, or the Hospital of St. George. The Brotherhood of Holy Charity was organized about the year 1450; but when two centuries had passed, its church and buildings had fallen into ruin and disuse. In 1661 one of the brethren, Don Miguel Mañara Vicentelo de Leca, a knight of Calatrava, determined to elevate it from its forlorn desolation, and set about raising funds to restore the buildings. In eighteen years he secured over half a million ducats, from bequests and donations. With this immense sum he erected a great cloistered hospital, in classic architecture, with one of the most beautiful churches in Seville, rich in sumptuous altars and costly plate and candelabra, and adorned with a lofty dome. He was also careful to retain so large an amount of money that permanent endowments were founded for the support of a large company of priests and sisters of charity, physicians, and domestics, so that even to the present day La Caridad is a fountain of beneficence. Thus the inscription which Mañara caused to be cut on the façade of the hospital is still true: "This house will stand as long as God shall be feared in it, and Jesus Christ be served in the persons of His poor. Whoever enters here must leave at the door both avarice and pride."

Mañara had been suddenly converted from a life of immorality to a profound devotion to the saints and to alms-giving; and had rigidly mortified his dearest fleshly lust, which was a remarkable fondness for chocolate. Miracles were wrought for him; and he caused many of his fellow-nobles to join the Brotherhood, and pour out their wealth in charity. This knightly philanthropist was a personal friend of Murillo, whom he commissioned to execute the artistic decoration of the new Church of St. George, at La Caridad. The master devoted four years to this work, painting eight pictures for the sidewalls, and three for the altars; for which he received 78,115 reals, or about $4,000.

The Casa Capitular of La Caridad still enshrines, as a precious relic, an autograph letter of Murillo, asking admission to the confraternity of pious and charitable men who bore the cares of the hospital.

The outer front of the Church of St. George is adorned with five large designs from the master's drawings, wrought in blue glazed tiles, after a bright Moorish fashion of decoration which had frequently been followed on the towers and gateways of Seville. The centre-piece represents Charity, with smaller sections on either side portraying Faith and Hope, and the knightly figures of Santiago and St. George below.

The series of eight pictures painted for the inner side walls treats of subjects appropriate to the place, and includes the noblest works of Murillo. Here he seems to have determined to leave an illuminated record of his versatility and vigor, in their fullest development. Bermudez says that if a set of careful engravings of these works had been made, they would have become as famous as the best achievements of Italian art. But now, scattered as they are in widely separated cities, no opportunity can be enjoyed of studying them as a series, and amid their proper surroundings. The picture of Moses shows the greatest intellectual power and the highest skill in conception and invention; but the Prodigal's Return and the St. Elizabeth were considered by Bermudez the finest of the group, in their more careful finish and richer coloring.

Three only of the eight pictures remain at La Caridad, the others having been carried to France by Marshal Soult, "the Plunder-master-general of Napoleon." These three represent Moses Striking the Rock, the Miracle of the Loaves and Fishes, and the Charity of San Juan de Dios. The first two are in a light and sketchy manner, though marvellous in composition; and the San Juan is full of rich and splendid color. In the first we see the noble figure of Moses, robed in violet drapery, with a full white beard and the traditional horn-shaped halo, standing in adoration beside the huge brown rock in Horeb, while groups of Israelites are eagerly drinking from the flowing stream. Aaron stands behind, astounded by the miracle; and around the two stately brethren are gathered fifteen men, women, and children, quenching their terrible thirst so ravenously that a mother even turns away from her clamorous child in her absorption. To the left are nine other figures, among whom a mother gives the full cup to her boy, and restrains with her hand his elder brother. This group is diversified by dogs and sheep, a patient-faced camel, and a white mule, drinking from an iron pot. The brown boy on the mule, and the pitcher-bearing girl near him, are said to be portraits of the master's children. In the background another company of people and animals is descending from the arid and rocky hills towards the water. The focal point is the great rock, reaching the top of the canvas and dividing the picture into two sections, before which is the erect figure of Moses, looking upward in a thanksgiving which contrasts strongly with the eager absorption of the people. Every head in all these grandly composed groups is worthy of study and admiration.

The Miracle of the Loaves and Fishes is less impressive than the scene in Horeb, lacking a sufficient elevation of character. Its most striking features are not in the apostolic group, as might have been expected, but among the people, — a young mother and her child, an incredulous and wondering old hag, and the lad with the loaves and fishes. Between the group of Christ and his followers on one side and a knot of spectators on the other, the great multitude is seen on the distant slopes. Marshal Soult owned a fine replica of this picture; and the original sketch is in the Munro Collection.

M. Thoré, in his *Études sur la Peinture Espagnole*, says, "If Christ fed five thousand men with five loaves and two fishes, Murillo painted five thousand men in a space of twenty-six feet. Truly, not one of the five thousand is absent; for there is an unheard-of multitude of women and children, of young men and old, a cloud of heads and arms moving at ease, without confusion, noise, or constraint. All are gazing at Christ among His disciples; and Christ blesses the bread, and the miracle is achieved. Magnificent teaching of charity, which the painter has magnificently set forth!"

The Charity of San Juan de Dios is perhaps

the best of the three pictures, and was highly commended by Sir David Wilkie. It shows the tender-hearted Father of the Poor, "the Good Samaritan of Granada," bearing a sick man on his shoulders through the darkness, and sinking under the heavy weight. He looks back with gratitude and awe to an angel who comes to aid him, lighting the gloom of the night and the sombre and suffering group with the glorious brilliancy of his face and his radiant robes. The execution of this work is spirited and powerful, and recalls the manner of Spagnoletto.

The great picture called *El Tiñoso* was removed from La Caridad of Seville by Marshal Soult, and is now in the Madrid Academy. It shows the saintly Queen Elizabeth of Hungary, with her crown over her white tissue veil, while she bends to wash the sores on the head of a leprous boy. Around her are groups of disgusting diseased beggars, mingled with exquisitely beautiful ladies of the royal court. Murillo painted many pictures of this class, illustrating the Spanish fascination for penitential charity, of which he found abundant models in every street of Seville. These subjects allowed or even forced the artist to mark the strongest contrast between blooming health and ghastly sickness, brilliant costumes of queens and squalid rags of mendicants.

Cean Bermudez says of the Tiñoso picture, that the Queen Elizabeth is equal to Van Dyck's best work, the boy's face is worthy of Paul Veronese, and the old woman recalls Velazquez. The composition and coloring of the whole design are admirable, and the rich contrasts in lights and shades are still apparent, in spite of the excessive restoration which the picture has suffered. The disgusting appearance of the ulcerous beggars, apparently as offensive to the queen's ladies as to the spectator, heightens the moral effect of the scene, and commands admiration for the pale and unshrinking Elizabeth, and for those who follow her in tender charity and helpfulness toward unfortunate humanity.

The pictures of Abraham Receiving the Angels, and the Prodigal's Return, were stolen from La Caridad by Marshal Soult, and were purchased from him by the Duke of Sutherland, in whose London residence of Stafford House they still remain. The first shows the grave and dignified patriarch, in dark robes and a turban, greeting the three supernatural visitors as they approach his tent. Bermudez and Stirling alike point out and lament the blemish of this picture in the deficient grace and dignity of the angels.

The Return of the Prodigal is a better composition, in which the pale and emaciated youth is folded in the arms of his father, while attendants lead in the fatted calf and bear the gold ring and the new robe of light blue silk. A pleasant touch of nature is seen in the little white dog, which is leaping upward, as if to crave caresses from his rehabilitated master.

"The Healing of the Paralytic" was bought from Marshal Soult in 1847, for $32,000, and is now owned by Mr. Tomline of London. The chief figures are those of Christ, three apostles, and the sick man, while the radiant angel who troubled the water of Bethesda is seen above, and in the background is a group of afflicted patients, in a series of beautiful arcades, like those of the Sevillian Convent of Mercy. The head of Christ is one of the noblest that Murillo ever executed, full of dignity and power; and the shoulder of the paralytic has for centuries been famous for its anatomical accuracy. The soft violet hue, so dear to Valencian art, of the Saviour's robe, is skilfully opposed to the deep brown of St. Peter's mantle, a rich tint then and still made by Andalusian painters from beef-bones.

The last of the eight Caridad pictures is "The Release of St. Peter," which is now in the Hermitage Palace at St. Petersburg.

The venerable Apostle is seen seated on the dungeon-floor, newly awakened from slumber, and with his face filled with amazement and gladness, and lighted by the glory which surrounds the delivering angel.

Stirling laments the dispersion of these pictures, and their degradation from incentives to piety to articles of furniture, in the following graphic sentences, whose underlying principle is of equal application to all similar works: "On the walls of the Spanish Academy, or of mansions in Paris or London, they have lost the voice with which they spoke to the heart from the altars of their native church. No poor patient, ere returning to the busy haunts of men, kneels now before the Healing of the Paralytic, in gratitude to Him who stood by the pool of Bethesda; no pale Sister of Charity, on her way to her labors of love in the hospital, implores the protection or is cheered by the example of the gentle St. Elizabeth. At Seville these pictures of charity were powerful and eloquent homilies, in which the piety of Miguel Mañara yet spake through the pencil of his friend. In the unfamiliar halls of the stranger they are now mere works of art, specimens of Murillo, articles of costly furniture, less esteemed perhaps, and less appropriate, than some Idalian glade imagined by Albano, some voluptuous Pompadour garden-scene, the offspring of Watteau."

CHAPTER VI.

Capuchin Pictures. — Trouble with Iriarte. — "The Children of the Shell." — "St. Ildefonso." — "St. Bernard's Vision."

BEFORE the Caridad pictures were finished, Murillo was engaged on the decoration of the new Capuchin church, which had been erected on an especially hallowed site, just beyond the walls of Seville. It is said that he dwelt for nearly three years in this convent, without once quitting it; and thereby the monks added to their famous ecclesiastical library the largest collection then extant of Murillo's paintings, including twenty pictures in which the figures were of life-size, besides several smaller works. Nine of these were framed on the *retablo* of the high altar; and eight were on the side-altars. They were saved from the march to Paris by the suspicious foresight of the monks, who sent them to Cadiz on the approach of the French army, where they lay stored until Napoleon's wars were ended. Seventeen of them are now in the Seville Museum, where they were placed at the time of the abolition of the convents.

A recent writer (Baxley's "Spain") states that Murillo's long sojourn in the Capuchin Convent was caused by his fear of the Inquisition, whose officers were on his track, but hesitated at taking him from the hospitality and protection of the powerful brotherhood with which he had found refuge. The alleged crime of the master consisted in his having portrayed the Virgin Mary with bare feet, which was a glaring violation of Pacheco's regulations. Baxley advances this statement with great confidence; but I cannot trace any allusion to such an event to an earlier date than 1875.

The Capuchin pictures formed a great series of harmonious works, full of truth and vigor, and imbued with the earnest spirit of the *naturalistas*. They were executed in the decade of Murillo's grandest achievements, between 1670 and 1680, and are illuminated by pure religious fervor.

The immense altar-piece is called *La Porciuncula*, and represents St. Francis kneeling on the rugged floor of his cavern, with Christ and the Madonna appearing to him. No less than thirty-three beautiful cherubim are seen above, showering the self-mortifying saint with red and white roses, which have arisen from the briers wherewith he scourged himself; "inculcating the moral, that as the roses of mundane delights have their thorns, so the thorns of pious austerity are not without their roses." In later days the foolish monks exchanged this picture for several inferior modern ones; and after passing through the hands of several owners, each of whom had it restored and repainted, it is now in the Madrid Museum.

In the same great carved frame-work over the high altar, were Murillo's beautiful pictures of Sts. Justa and Rufina, St. Anthony of Padua, St. John in the Desert, St. Joseph holding Jesus, St. Felix of Cantalicio, the Veronica, Sts. Leander and Bonaventure, and the Madonna.

The Sts. Justa and Rufina are here portrayed more beautifully than ever before; the St. John and the St. Joseph are full of majestic vigor and manliness; and the Sts. Leander and Bonaventure are grandly robed in white, and accompanied by a charming Correggiesque boy. But the gem of the altar-piece is the Madonna, — a small square picture, showing the innocent yet thoughtful face of Mary, with the Holy Child leaning forward almost out of the picture, as if to welcome Joseph the carpenter after a day of toil. The radiant light and brilliant coloring of this picture were never excelled, even by Murillo. There is a pleasant legend attached to this work, borne out by its size and shape, which has caused the Spaniards to name it "The Virgin of the Napkin" (*La Virgen de la Serviletta*). The lay-brother who acted as the cook of the convent was assiduous in his attentions to Murillo; and when the great paintings were finished, he asked him to leave with him a trifling memorial of his pencil. The master answered that he had no canvas left; upon which the quick-witted cook handed him a napkin, asking him to paint on that. Ever anxious to make those around him happy, Murillo set to work on this square of coarse linen, and before nightfall had transformed it into a glorious treasure of art.

The great pictures at the lateral altars illustrated St. Thomas of Villanueva, St. Francis at the Cross, St. Anthony of Padua, the Vision of St. Felix, the Annunciation, the Immaculate Conception, the Nativity, and the Virgin with the dead Christ. The first-named is the finest of the series, and was esteemed by Murillo as the best of all his works. He used to call it *mi cuadro*, or his own picture; and its subject was so pleasing to him, that he made several paintings of the same scene, two of which are now in England, and a third at the Louvre. In this, the most elaborate and successful of all, the venerable and dignified St. Thomas, Archbishop of Valencia, is distributing alms at the door of his cathedral, with a picturesque group of ragged beggars expectantly waiting. His pale yet loving face indicates the rigor of his austerities towards himself, and the breadth of his good-will to all mankind.

"St. Francis at the Cross" illustrates a legend of the *Flos Sanctorum* concerning an apparition of Christ to the seraphic saint in his grotto on Mount Alvernus, when He inflicted on him the wounds of the stigmata. The saint is filled with ecstasy, and upholds the body of the Saviour, Who is nailed to the cross by one hand, while He rests the other on His follower's shoulder.

The picture of St. Anthony of Padua depicts

that holy man kneeling, and perusing a great open folio, on which the Infant Jesus has placed Himself.

"The Vision of St. Felix of Cantalicio" shows that holy and self-mortified monk laying the Infant Christ in the arms of the Virgin, after having embraced Him tenderly. The tradition states that this celestial vision occurred in Rome, a few hours before the death of the saint.

"The Immaculate Conception" in this series is similar in design to another and far superior work on the same theme, painted for the same church, save that it has the Eternal Father in its upper part, and Satan, in the form of a dragon, below. The other is a radiant work, with the Virgin standing on a bank of clouds upheld by lovely cherub-children, while she looks upward in adoration. She is in the bloom of youth, with fair hair and wide blue eyes.

"The Nativity" was highly extolled by Cean Bermudez, and the Virgin therein is one of Murillo's most exquisite works. Her sweet and loving face is illuminated with light emanating from the new-born child, which falls also on the forms of St. Joseph and the shepherds near by.

Besides these larger works Murillo enriched the Capuchin Convent with several other pictures, among which were two of the Archangel Michael; a Crucifixion, painted on the wooden altar-cross; and "The Guardian Angel." The latter illustrates the Catholic idea that every soul has an angelic protector through the pilgrimage of the world. It is a splendidly wrought allegory, full of sweetness and delicacy, and shows a gentle yet majestic angel, in a yellow robe and purple mantle, leading a young child, and pointing him to heaven. The diaphanous drapery of the child is notable as an innovation in Spanish art.

In 1814 the monks presented this picture to the Cathedral, being probably forewarned of the approaching dissolution of the convents, and wishing to save something for the Church. In that stately temple it still remains, as one of the jewels of Seville.

Several important pictures of Murillo's later years remain to be noticed briefly. It is impossible to ascertain their precise dates and chronological sequence, but they are nearly all in the *vaporoso* manner.

The Marquis of Villamanrique commissioned Murillo to illustrate the life of King David, in several large pictures.

He was at that time dubious of his ability to execute landscape backgrounds, and engaged Ignacio Iriarte to perform that part of the work. But Iriarte demanded that the figures should be done first, and the landscapes afterwards; an arrangement which Murillo could not sanction, and determined to execute the whole work himself. He changed the subject to the life of Jacob, and painted five large pictures, full of laborious painstaking and masterly skill, and furnished with the adjuncts of pastoral scenery, flocks, herds, and rude shepherds. These works remained in the Santiago Palace at Madrid until the War of Independence, when they were scattered. "Jacob Receiving Isaac's Blessing" and "Jacob's Dream" are now at St. Petersburg; "Jacob Placing the Peeled Wands before Laban's Cattle" was in the late Northwick Collection; and the Marquis of Westminster owns "Laban Seeking for his Gods in the Tent of Rachel." The Aguado Collection contained several other and smaller paintings from scenes in the life of

Jacob, whereof Jacob's Dream, his Combat with the Angel, and his Servitude with Laban have been engraved.

The rupture between Murillo and Iriarte was unfortunate; for they had previously been on intimate terms for many years, and had frequently executed joint works. Iriarte had devoted all his life to studying and painting landscapes along the Sierra Morena and in the Guadalquivir valley; and Murillo admired his works so highly that he said they were done by divine inspiration. A picture which was left unfinished when these comrades quarrelled still remains to prove that Iriarte had previously done what his friend desired him to do in the Jacob series; for here the landscape is finished around the barely sketched figures of Murillo's group. Iriarte has been called "The Spanish Claude Lorraine;" and his few remaining works are highly prized.

In 1672 the master painted portraits of Nicolas Omazurino and his wife, Isabel Malcampo. Nicolas was a warm friend of the artist, and lent him money; and after his death had a fine engraving made by Coilin, in Flanders, from the painting which Murillo had painted for his own children. He was originally from Antwerp, and appears to have been both wealthy and generous.

"Rebecca and Eliezer" is a composition of several figures of half life-size, now in the Madrid Museum, with the weary pilgrim drinking from Rebecca's pitcher, while his camels and servants approach from a distance. The hospitable maiden and her companions stand in the golden sunset, near an Andalusian village-fountain, with a range of mountains in the background. There is room for romantic conjecture as to whose face was the original model for that of Rebecca; for the same features appear in the pictures of the Miracle of Moses, and the Virgin of the Corsini Palace, and several times as one of the patronesses of Seville, Sts. Justa and Rufina.

The beautiful picture which the Spaniards call "The Children of the Shell," now at Madrid, shows the young St. John the Baptist holding a shell-full of water to the lips of Jesus. Nowhere is Murillo more at home than when painting children, whose life was his continual study and delight. The brown and jocund boys and girls of the Feria, ragged though they might be, were

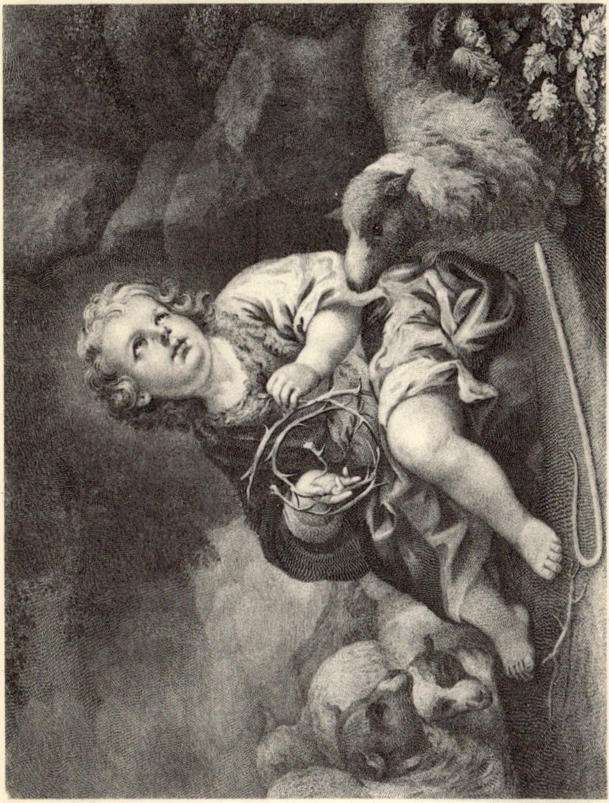

far more picturesque than Velazquez's pale princelings and dukelets; and the master made many sketches from them, which he afterwards refined and idealized into religious pictures of consummate interest. There are many pictures from his easel showing the youthful Jesus or St. John with lambs by their sides; commemorating the custom which is still prevalent at Seville, of each family buying a lamb for its Easter feast. Still in those ancient streets travellers meet the types of Murillo's St. Johns, dark-eyed and sun-browned urchins, playing in the sunshine with their Paschal lambs.

The great picture of "St. Ildefonso Receiving the Chasuble from the Virgin," now at the Madrid Museum, was probably executed about this time, and portrays the proudest legend of imperial Toledo. Ildefonso, the strenuous defender of the doctrine of the Immaculate Conception, once entered his Cathedral at the head of a midnight procession, and saw an intense and unsupportable light about the high altar. He alone dared to advance, and saw the Virgin sitting on his ivory throne, surrounded by chanting angels. She said, "Come hither, most faithful servant of God, and receive this robe which I have brought thee from the treasury of my Son;" and threw over him a miraculous chasuble, which was arranged by angelic choristers. The painting shows the moment of the investiture, with the lovely Virgin and angels; and the delicate embroidery on the chasuble has been delineated with minute care and brilliancy. This picture has been engraved by Selma.

"The Appearance of the Virgin to St. Bernard of Clairvaux" is another large religious picture of Murillo's best time, and is now in the Madrid Museum. The dignity and nobility of its treatment here redeem the infelicity of the legend. The white-robed saint is in his study, surrounded by huge old scholastic tomes, when Our Lady and her attendent cherubs appear to him; and, as he kneels before her, she causes a stream of milk to flow from her bosom upon his lips. Thencefoward no audience could resist the sweet and spiritual eloquence of the venerable saint, which was ever devoted to the service of the Queen of Heaven. This picture has been engraved by Muntaner. The figures in the original are of full length and life size, like those in the "St. Ildefonso."

The picture of St. Anna teaching the Virgin, formerly in the chapel of the Palace of St. Ildefonso, is now in the Madrid Museum, and portrays Mary kneeling by her mother's side in close attention. She is simply dressed, and her only ornament is a white rose embedded in her flowing golden tresses. The mother's head is noble and dignified; and the elaborate care with which both faces were executed, and their evident portrait character, has given rise to the supposition that they were painted from Doña Beatriz and Francisca, the wife and daughter of Murillo. The theme herein illustrated was unorthodox, as before shown, but was a great favorite with many artists.

CHAPTER VII.

The Nun-Daughter. — The Old Priests' Pictures. — Augustine Illustrated. — Murillo's Sickness. — His Will. — His Death.

IN 1676 Murillo's daughter Francisca bade farewell to the world, and entered the Convent of the Mother of God, a splendid establishment which had been founded by Isabella the Catholic, and enlarged by Archbishop de Deza. Probably there was some connection between the choice of her retreat and the fact that its most venerated nun was Sebastiana de Neve, a relative of Murillo's friend the Canon Justino Neve. Sebastiana had recently been delivered from a serious malady by the miraculous interposition of the beatified Peruvian, St. Rosa of Lima. According to tradition, Francisca was the model for the Madonnas in two pictures of the Immaculate Conception now in the Museums of Seville and Madrid, wherein the features are identical.

In 1678 the friendly canon, Don Justino Neve y Yevenes, was busily engaged in building the new Hospital de los Venerables, or asylum for aged priests, and summoned Murillo to decorate it with pictures. For the chapel he executed "The Repentance of St. Peter," a powerful work in the manner of Ribera; and "Our Lady of the Immaculate Conception," whose coloring excelled that of all his numerous representations of the same subject. The refectory was adorned with a picture of the Virgin and Child enthroned amid the clouds, with Jesus taking bread from a basket borne by angels, and giving it to three aged priests. This delightful composition, which some have preferred to all the other works of the artist, was placed where the ecclesiastical veterans could see it while they eat their daily meals. It was stolen by the French invaders, leaving but a poor reproduction in a copy at the Cadiz Museum. Another decoration of the refectory was a splendid full-length portrait of Canon Neve, executed by Murillo with all his skill as a tribute of gratitude and admiration. This is now carefully preserved at Bowood, the mansion of the Marquis of Lansdowne. It is clearly and carefully painted, and shows a delicate olive face, refined and pleasing, with intelligent dark eyes;

and the comfortable and respectable canon is robed in a black cassock, and sits in a red velvet chair. The sleek spaniel at his feet is so admirably portrayed that dogs have been heard to snarl and bark as they approached it.

The next work on which the master engaged was a series of paintings from the life of St. Augustine, for the Augustinian convent-church. His friend Pedro de Medina had recently repaired and regilt the high altar, and advised the monks to adorn it with pictures by Seville's greatest master. Two of these are now in the Museum of the city, and show the appearance of the Madonna to St. Augustine, and the same saint writing in solitude. A third picture is now in the Louvre, and illustrates the legend of St. Augustine and the child by the seashore. The same convent also contained two scenes from the life of St. Thomas of Villanueva.

In 1679 Murillo's tried and trusty friend Mañara died, bequeathing his fortune to the hospital of La Caridad. He was honored with a pompous funeral, and was buried in the Church of St. George, whose walls had been hung with Murillo's paintings under his direction.

During the later years of Murillo, he was in the habit of making frequent visits to the Church of Santa Cruz, in his parish, where he spent many hours and offered earnest prayers before the altar-piece of "The Descent from the Cross." This grand picture was painted by Pedro Campaña, a century earlier, in the formal Florentine manner. Pacheco declared that he was afraid to remain alone with it at twilight, so terrible was its realistic power. As Murillo was lingering here late in the dusk, one day, he answered the sacristan's challenge by saying: "I am waiting till those men have brought the body of Our Blessed Lord down the ladder."

Murillo's last work was a large altar-piece for the Capuchin Church at Cadiz, representing "The Betrothal of St. Catherine," for which he was to have received 700 crowns. He had already finished the figures of the Madonna and Child and St. Catherine, when, one day, as he was climbing a scaffolding to work on the upper section of the picture, he stumbled violently, and ruptured himself. The ancient Spanish writers do not state where this accident occurred; but tradition claims that it was in the chapel of the

Capuchin Convent at Cadiz, where the fatal picture still remains. Stirling, however, thinks that it must have happened in his studio at Seville, and points out how nearly impossible it would have been for a person so badly injured to be transported over the rugged road or up the tedious river to Seville, where he died.

Palomino says that the master's shrinking modesty would not allow him to reveal the nature of his injury. But he continued to grow worse, and soon perceived that his earthly course was nearly ended. He summoned his notary, Juan Antonio Guerrero, and drew up his will; but death advanced so rapidly that he was unable to consummate the necessary legal formalities, or even to sign the document.

The will is still preserved, and begins with the following solemn sentences: —

"In the name of God, Amen: Let it be known to as many as this letter of testament shall reach, that I, Bartolomé Murillo, master of the art of painting, citizen of this city of Seville, in the precinct of Santa Cruz, being infirm of body and sound in will and in all deliberate judgment and natural understanding, full and good memory, such as God Our Lord has vouchsafed to give me, and believing as I do firmly and truly in the divine mystery of the Holy Trinity, Father, Son, and Holy Spirit, three persons really distinct and yet one true God, and in all the rest which the holy mother, the Roman Catholic Church, holds, believes, and confesses, as a Christian desiring salvation, and wishing to be prepared for that which God Our Lord may be pleased to dispose, and taking as I do the ever Virgin Mary Our Lady for my intercessor, conceived without stain or affinity to original sin from the first instant of her existence, I make and order my testament in the following manner: —

"Firstly: I offer and commit my soul to God Our Lord, who created it and redeemed it with the infinite price of His blood, of whom I humbly supplicate to pardon it, and bear it to peace in glory; and, when His divine majesty is pleased to remove me from this life, I command that my body be buried in my parish-church, and that there may be said for my soul the chanted requiem that is customary; and the form and disposition of my burial I leave to the judgment of my executors. Item: I order that four hundred masses shall be said for my soul, the fourth part of them in my parish-church, a hundred in the convent of Our Lady of Mercy, a great house of this city, and the rest in the convents and places which my executors may choose; and that the alms may be paid as is customary."

He further orders that the articles of silver plate which he had inherited from his cousin Maria, the widow of Don Francisco Terron, should be sold, and the proceeds thereof should be invested in masses for her soul. 50 reals are bequeathed to his servant Anna Maria de Salcedo, "to be delivered as soon as I die." He states that the notary Andres de Campo of Pilas owes him 2,000 reals for the rent of his olive-yards for four years; and orders the collection of the debt, deducting 180 reals for ten arrobas of oil which he had received from Campo. Again he speaks of rent due from his houses in the parish of La Magdalena, at the rate of eight ducats each. The advance of 350 crowns which the Capuchins of Cadiz had made on his last picture is alluded to; and provision is made for the delivery of certain new paintings to their owners. After all debts were paid, the remainder of the estate was to revert to the sons of the testator, Gabriel and Gaspar.

The fatal hernia soon accomplished its work; and at six o'clock in the evening of April 3, 1682, the master died, drawing his last breath while supported in the arms of his old friend Canon Neve, and his scholar Pedro Nuñez de Villavicencio. His young son Gaspar, then in priest's orders, was present at the bedside.

The funeral of Murillo was conducted with great pomp, as befitted the memory of the illustrious dead. The bier was carried by two marquises and four knights, and followed by a great assembly of mourning citizens of all ranks. At his request, he was buried beneath his favorite picture, Campaña's " Descent from the Cross," in a chapel of the Church of Santa Cruz; and on the stone slab over his remains were carved his name, a skeleton, and the words, —

VIVE MORITVRVS.

While Marshal Soult held Seville, the French pillaged and destroyed the Church of Santa Cruz, leaving on its site only a heap of weedy rubbish. Its site is now occupied by the Plaza of Santa Cruz; and a tablet, placed in an adjacent wall in

1858, commemorates the fact that Murillo was buried here.

Elsewhere the city of Seville has honored the memory of one of her noblest sons, by erecting a stately bronze statue of Murillo on the Plaza del Museo, near the Provincial Museum, in which so many of his pictures are preserved.

CHAPTER VIII.

Murillo's Style. — His Madonnas. — *Genre*-Painting. — The Beggar-Pictures. — Portraits. — Landscapes. — Limitations.

The grand trio of Spanish artists who preceded Murillo were the monkish Zurbaran, the gloomy Ribera, and the portrait-painter Velazquez. As the latter was pre-eminent among the court-painters, so Murillo held the supremacy among the ecclesiastical painters, in variety and versatility as well as in thorough knowledge of all the departments of his profession. His art was multiform in its inspirations and manifestations, and was pervaded by the clear light of a strong personality.

He blended in his style all the peculiar beauties of the school of Andalusia, — its richness and depth of tone, its light and fleecy clouds, fresh flowers and sparkling waters, backgrounds of rugged sierras, and the red and brown tints so universal on the lower Guadalquivir. Another traditional excellency of the Andalusian artists was their skilful and graceful management of drapery, in which their great chief was unsurpassed.

Murillo, considered as a religious painter, is second only to the great masters of Italy; and yields to them even, mainly in ideality and grace. They, indeed, had the advantage of the study of the masterpieces of antiquity; but he was practically debarred from such inspirations, and left to develop an independent manner. "Athenian sculpture of the age of Pericles therefore had, directly at least, no more to do with the formation of his taste than the Mexican painting of the age of Montezuma. All his ideas were of home growth; his mode of expression was purely national and Spanish; his model, nature as it existed in and around Seville."

His gentle and amiable spirit reflected itself in his paintings, giving an unwonted tenderness and sweetness to the religious art of Spain, which had hitherto been almost savage in its penances and self-mortifications. Mariolatry was then (as it still is) almost the only religion in Spain, and the artists of the peninsula were all employed in portraying the object of the national adoration.

Even the saints received but occasional notice; and the other Persons connected with the Christian system were rarely represented, except as adjuncts of the Madonna.

Murillo's Madonnas are paradoxical creations, strangely combining a mystic conception and a realistic execution, marvellously brilliant, yet not altogether comprehensible. Their difference from the pictures of the Italian artists is radical, and in opposite directions; since in one class of subjects they were more naturalistic, and in another more supernatural, in treatment. The Tuscan and Venetian schools deemed it incumbent on their artists to show their respect for the Mother of God, by portraying her as an inhabitant of such a splendid palace as would have astonished all Syria, with luxurious accompaniments and good Catholic prie-dieux and missals. In the scenes of her beatification, she is usually surrounded by unearthly cherubs' heads, winged and mystic, and connected in the view with groups of saints and apostles, thoroughly natural and comprehensible. But Murillo marks a broader contrast by depicting her earthly life, with close fidelity to the Gospels, as that of a Galilean peasant-dame, in the midst of suggestions of domestic life. In the later scenes Murillo adopts a peculiar mode of treatment, as regards the Assumption and the miraculous apparitions of the Madonna, showing her as an imponderable being, floating in ethereal spaces, surrounded by a profound glory, and standing on a crescent moon no larger than a sickle. About her play countless cherubic infants, plump-limbed and joyful, idealized human children, tumbling over each other on the massive silvery clouds, and receding into the golden light in the background. Some bear white lilies, roses, palms, and olive-branches, or sceptres and crowns, and hover triumphantly in the sunny air, giving an exuberant life to contrast with the statuesque repose of the Virgin. The blooming roses and lilies in the hands of the cherubs are painted with as perfect finish, and in as exquisite beauty, as the pure and rapturous face of the Elect Lady, "spotless without, and innocent within."

"Never has dignified composure and innocence of mind, unruffled by human guilt or passion, heavenly beatitude past utterance, or the unconquerable majesty and 'hidden strength of chastity, been more exquisitely portrayed She appears in a state of ecstatic beatitude, and borne aloft in a golden æther to heaven, to which her beauteous eyes are turned, by a group of angels, which none could color like him. The retiring virgin loveliness of the Blessed Mary seems to have stolen so gently, so silently, on her, that she is unaware of her own power and fascination."

As a *genre*-painter, Murillo achieved many notable triumphs, especially in connection with the portrayal of the life of the lower classes. One of his most successful works in this department was the *Las Gallegas*, showing a young and smiling maiden leaning on a window-sill, with an older and less comely woman behind her. The picture of these frail fair ones remained in the family of the Dukes of Almodovar until 1823, when the estate was broken up on the failure of the male line, and *Las Gallegas* was bought by the British Ambassador, and sent to Heytesbury Hall, in Wiltshire. A repetition of it is in Munro's gallery at Novar, Fifeshire. "The Old Spinster," now at Madrid, is a powerful study of a wrinkled crone plying her distaff; and "The Gallician of the Money," in the same Museum, is a brown gypsy girl, with wild bright eyes and pearly teeth.

Murillo painted not only the noble and stately themes of Spanish and Latin religion, and celestial apparitions of the Queen of Heaven, but also the most plebeian and mundane subjects, with a surprising equality of interest and care. It was characteristic and natural for Spanish artists to portray solemn Madonnas and ecstatic saints; but their great chief held this ground with unsurpassable power, and added to it the ability and enjoyment of painting vermicidal beggar-boys, squalid and sun-steeped lazzaroni, frowsy flower-girls, and brown and ragamuffin gypsies. And why not — if the mission of art is to ennoble and idealize the scenes of daily life and experience? for how few were those who could even think of the Immaculate Conception, while the teeming life of the sidewalks and suburbs was the foremost fact in Seville!

There was no contempt in Murillo's feelings towards these children of Nature; and his sentiments seemed to partake almost of a fraternal sympathy for them. No small portion of his popularity among the lower classes arose from the

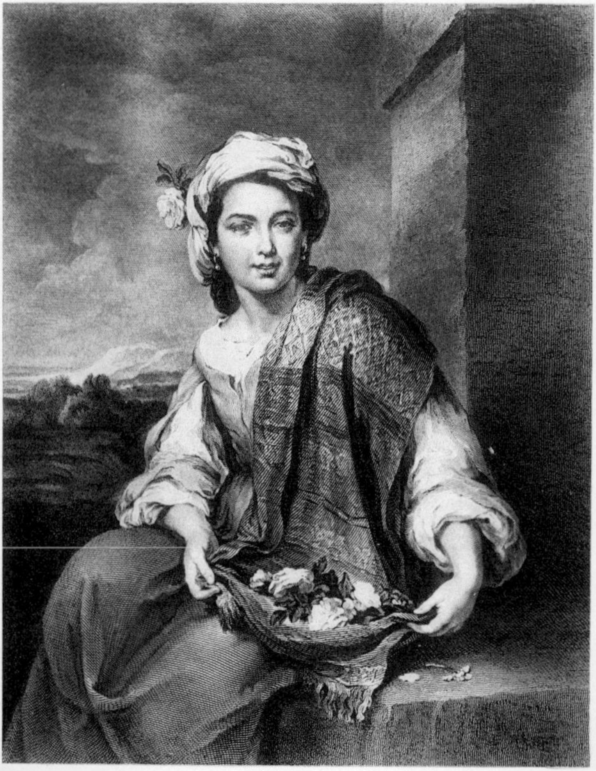

knowledge that he was their poet and court-painter, who understood and did not calumniate them. Velazquez had chosen to paint superb dukes and cardinals, and found his supporters in a handful of supercilious grandees; but Murillo illustrated the lives of the poorest classes on Spanish soil, and was the idol of the masses.

With what splendor of color and mastery of design did he thus illuminate the annals of the poor! Coming forth from some dim chancel or palace-hall in which he had been working on a majestic Madonna-picture, he would sketch in, with the brush still loaded with the colors of celestial glory, the lineaments of the beggar crouching by the wall, or the gypsy calmly reposing in the black shadow of the archway. Such versatility had never before been seen west of the Mediterranean, and commanded the admiration of his countrymen.

We do not find in his pictures the beggar of Britain and America, cold, lowering, gloomy, and formidable; but the laughing child of the sunlight, full of joy and content, preferring to bask rather than to work, yet always fed somehow, and abundantly; crop-haired, brown-footed, clad in incoherent rags, but bright-eyed, given to much joviality, and with an affluence of white teeth, often shown in merry moods; not so respectable as the staid burghers of Nuremberg and Antwerp, but far more picturesque, and perhaps quite as happy; now passing wealthy in owning a melon or a bunch of grapes; now as lordly as a grandee, in patronizing some faithful but mangy dog; now sanguinary as the Great Captain himself, in long campaigns among the hairs of a comrade's head, — but ever jocund and healthy, and a good Catholic.

As a portrait-painter Murillo occupied a very high rank, and showed with what profit he had studied the masterpieces of the illustrious Velazquez. Among the few portraits which he executed were the famous ones of Pedro Cavanillas, the Carmelite monk, now at Madrid; the Archbishop Pedro de Urbina, who was buried in the Franciscan Convent in 1663; and the philanthropist Miguel Mañara. The Louvre contains three valuable portraits, the first representing Murillo's aged servant, Anna de Salcedo, bearing a pestle and mortar; the second is a wrinkled old woman, called the mother of the artist; and the other shows the unprepossessing full-length figure of Don Andres de Andrade, painted in a forcible and realistic manner, and accompanied by a large and unamiable white mastiff.

Murillo ranks as a landscape-painter next to Velazquez, but lacks the vividness and clearness of that master. His scenery is graceful, but conventional; and rests in pale gray lights, lacking in brilliancy and richness of tone. Two companion-pictures in the Madrid Museum depict a rocky highland country, through which flows a river, with a fortress and a bridge. The Aguado Collection contained the largest number of the master's landscapes ever brought together.

It is worthy of note and of wonder, that Murillo never painted a historical scene, or illustrated a secular tradition, though Spaniards are so proud of their heroic annals, and the southern provinces were so rich in records and legends of the Moorish wars. In his day the Chronicles of the Cid and the "Seville Restaurada" were in all men's mouths; the grass had hardly yet had time to grow on Cervantes' grave; and Lope de Vega and Calderon were still living, and writing myriads of dramas. He equally disregarded the brilliant and picturesque scenes of the discovery and conquest of America, many of whose heroes were then dwelling about him. How gladly would the moderns exchange one of his multitudinous Conception-pictures for a delineation of the exodus of the Moorish tribes from Andalusia, or a scene in the dread epoch when the Inquisition drowned the southern reformation in the blood of martyred Spaniards, or a glimpse of Ponce de Leon marching through Florida!

Another singular fact in Murillo's art-life is that he never painted a mythological picture, though he might well have been led in that direction by the tempting Venuses of Titian which he had seen at Madrid. The study of classic statuary, which had formed so prominent a feature with the artists of Italy, was impossible in his case, for Spain was almost devoid of antiques. There was a petty collection at Alcalá, but no one knows that he ever visited it.

Let us hear Viardot's earnest words: "Murillo comes up, in every respect, to what our imagination could hope or conceive. His earthly daylight is perfectly natural and true; his heavenly day is full of radiance. We find in the attitude of the saints, and the expression of their features, all that the most ardent piety, all that the most passionate exaltation, can feel or express in extreme surprise, delight, and adoration. As for the visions, they appear with all the pomp of a celestial train, in which are marvellously grouped the different spirits of the immortal hierarchy, from the archangel with outspread wings to the bodiless heads of the cherubim. It is in these scenes of supernatural poetry that the pencil of Murillo, like the wand of an enchanter, produces marvels. If, in scenes taken from human life, he equals the greatest colorists, he is alone in the imaginary scenes of eternal life. It might be said of the two great Spanish masters, that Velazquez is the painter of the earth, and Murillo of heaven."

CHAPTER IX.

Spanish Art and Seclusion. — Soult. — Collections of Murillo's Works. — Drawings. — Murillo and Velazquez. — Later Artists of Spain.

The art of Italy was evolved from the crude cold manner of the Byzantine painters by centuries of slow development; and that of Germany was hampered by ungracious Gothic traditions, which long checked its advance. But Spanish art reached its maturity at once, since it had no ancient errors to correct, and could avail itself directly of the fruits of foreign labors. It rose late, but attained an excellence which has only been surpassed by the divinest of Italy's artists. Nearly all the eminent painters of Spain, and hundreds of those now forgotten, studied in Italy during the period between the rise of Raphael and the death of Tintoretto.

Yet how little is known of the art of Spain, the China of Christendom! Nearly three centuries ago Domenichino gave way to tumultuous grief when he heard that one of Titian's finest pictures had been sent to Madrid; as if it had gone beyond the ken of Christian man. In the second quarter of the nineteenth century, Sir David Wilkie called Spain "the Timbuctoo of artists," an unknown and almost unknowable realm. Nearly two millenniums before, the classic poet had characterized it, in rueful apostrophe, *O dura tellus Iberiæ;* and Strabo stigmatized its people as αφιλοκαλια, or without the love of beauty.

The free march of French armies throughout the peninsula, in the days of the First Napoleon, brought about an extension of the fame of Spanish art; for their retreating baggage-trains carried into Northern Europe hundreds of priceless paintings. During this and the succeeding wars, the jealous seclusion of the palaces of the grandees and the cloisters of the hierarchs was broken, and their mouldering art-treasures were brought to view. In 1779 Charles III. forbade the exportation of Murillo's pictures, so indifferent had the people become as to their public value. Nevertheless, with the curious national instinct of retaining jealously, even while not appreciating, those things which have been bequeathed from former generations (in our days, the island of Cuba), the nobles and clergy held their pictures grimly, so that Cumberland wrote, in 1782, that they would "never be extracted from the country, as they are in the palaces."

The stream of Raphael's pictures, borne north from Italy on the limbers of the French generals, mingled at Paris with a similar current of the masterpieces of Spanish art. Marshal Soult was especially energetic in plundering southern Spain of its best pictures, from whose sale he derived great sums in after years. It is related that he was once showing his gallery to a British officer, and, stopping before a fine Murillo, he said, "I very much value *that*, as it saved the lives of two estimable persons." An attendant aide-de-camp explained this mysterious assertion by whispering to the visitor, "He threatened to have both shot on the spot, unless they *gave* up the picture."

Marshal Soult's robberies were skilfully planned and premeditated; and the cities in advance of his army were explored by spies, in the disguise of tourists, who were provided with

Cean Bermudez's Dictionary of Art in Spain, and marked out the richest treasures of plate and pictures. The Marshal seized the objects of his covetousness, and carefully guarded the legality of their titles by forcing their owners to sign fictitious bills of sale. These trophies were transferred to Soult's house in Paris; and for many years afterwards the thrifty veteran derived a large income from selling them, one by one, to wealthy English nobles. Hundreds of other pictures had been huddled into the Alcazar of Seville, awaiting transportation to France; but the sudden retreat of the French army compelled their abandonment.

Murillo, like Velazquez, early came into the sunshine of a high contemporary fame, and dwelt there in unassailed possession and peace. No Spanish painter was better known in foreign lands; and even in his own day his pictures were esteemed in Italy, England, and the Netherlands. His portrait was engraved in Flanders during the last year of his life; and in the next year his was the only Spanish name in the German Sandrart's great Latin folio on artists, where a laudatory but inaccurate biography is given.

So untiring was Murillo's industry, and so rapid was his pencil, that by the close of the seventeenth century there was scarcely a church or convent in the province, or a respectable house in Seville, that did not possess one or more of his works. When the first Bourbon king of Spain, Philip V., visited the city, early in the last century, many of these pictures were acquired by the noblemen in the royal train, and removed elsewhere.

Indeed, the demand for the master's pictures began at an early date; for, not to speak of the rude works sent westward in the caravels of Cadiz, they are recorded as having passed into France and Italy even during his life. In 1693 Evelyn, the dashing cavalier of Wotton, writes in his Memoirs, with an air of amazement, that a certain English nobleman had recently "bought the picture of the Boys, by Morillio, the Spaniard, for eighty guineas."

The choicest collections of Murillo's pictures are still at Seville in the Museum and La Caridad, with several in private collections. The Madrid Museum has a large number also; but they are not his finest specimens, and do not afford the best studies of his manner. The Louvre has a remarkably large and varied collection, some of which were purchased, and others stolen by the armies of Napoleon. Germany preserves several choice works, in various galleries; and the Hermitage Palace at St. Petersburg contains nearly thirty, some of which are very celebrated. The British nobility and amateurs have been possessed with a rage for Murillo's paintings, and have bought them with lavish prodigality. Many spurious copies, closely imitating the master's *vaporoso* manner, have been palmed off on these enthusiasts; and many noble originals have been picked up by connoisseurs in remote parts of Andalusia. The Government bought the picture of St. John for $10,000, and placed it in the National Gallery. Dulwich College also has a large and brilliant collection of fine works by Murillo, including some undoubted masterpieces. Dozens of the splendid castles and country-seats of Old England have rich productions of the pencil of the great Sevillian master.

The largest sale of Murillo's pictures occurred in the year 1843, when the Aguado Collection was dispersed. No less than fifty-five compositions of the great master were disposed of at this time. In 1852 Marshal Soult's collection was sold, and the fifteen Murillos which it contained brought $232,649. At this sale the French Government bought the Madonna of the Immaculate Conception, which is now in the Louvre, for $123,060.

The Louvre contains twenty-two drawings by Murillo, small and neatly finished with pen and ink, and washed over with a solution of licorice. These were once possessed by the Count of Aguila; and two more sketches from the same source are in Ford's collection, at Heavitree, Devonshire. The finest of these, and the most beautiful of the artist's drawings, is a large design of the Crucifixion, carefully executed in colored crayons. Mr. Ford also possesses the only known etching of the master, representing St. Francis at the foot of the cross.

Andalusia and Castile found the flowering of their artistic genius in Murillo and Velazquez; and the most successful painters of later years were those who followed their methods the most closely. Velazquez worked slowly and leisurely, with wealthy patrons and a good salary, and fin-

ished his pictures with deliberation and care, to meet the criticism of the connoisseurs of the royal court. But Murillo was constantly employed on large works for monks and ecclesiastics ignorant of the requirements of technical excellence, and therefore paid less attention to the refinement of details.

In one point, at least, Murillo and Velazquez were united in sympathy, and that was the thoroughly Spanish character of their works. There is, indeed, an intense national spirit running through the lives and productions of the artists of the peninsula, manifesting itself most clearly in their close imitation of real nature in Spain.

A comparison between Velazquez and Murillo is inevitably demanded by the circumstances of their mutual relations, and cannot be given better than in the words of Sir David Wilkie, a close student of both artists: "Velazquez has more intellect and expression, more to surprise and captivate the artist. Murillo has less power, but a higher aim in coloring; in his flesh he has an object distinct from most of his contemporaries, and seems, like Rembrandt, to aim at the general character of flesh when tinged with the light of the sun. His color seems adapted for the higher style of art; it is never minute or particular, but a general and poetical recollection of nature. For female and infantile beauty, he is the Correggio of Spain. Velazquez, by his high technical excellence, is the delight of all artists; Murillo, adapting the higher subjects of art to the commonest understanding, seems, of all painters, the most universal favorite. . . .

"Velazquez and Murillo are preferred, and preferred with reason, to all the others, as the most original and characteristic of their school. These two great painters are remarkable for having lived in the same time, in the same school, painted from the same people, and yet to have formed two styles so different and opposite, that the most unlearned can scarcely mistake them; Murillo being all softness, while Velazquez is all sparkle and vivacity."

After Murillo's death the standards of Spanish art were rapidly lowered, nor could the moribund Academy of Seville check the fatal decadence. When Raphael Mengs, "the incarnation of the academical mediocre," came to Spain, eighty years later, the art of the peninsula was ready for burial. The traditions of Seville were upheld in monotonous beauty of numerous Madonnas of Guadaloupe, by Cabrera, Ximenes, and other talented artists of the Mexican school, whose lives were dedicated to the decoration of the cloisters under the Rocky Mountains.

Murillo had twelve or more disciples, the chief of whom were Miguel de Tobar, Menesis Orio, and Pedro Nuñez de Villavicencio. These followed the master's footsteps afar off; and several of the *genre*-pictures which are now attributed to Murillo were doubtless executed by these pupils. But such reflected merit could not arrest the speedy and final fall of Andalusian art, which came before the close of the century.

The art of Castile fell into a deep sleep when the last contemporary imitator of Velazquez died. When the Spanish kings wanted painters, they were forced to import them. Charles II. sent to Italy for Luca Giordano, Philip V. to France for Ranc and Houasse, and Charles III. called to his court the German Raphael Mengs. At last one more grand genius arose, and took up the fallen pencil of Velazquez. This was Francisco Goya y Lucientes, the Hogarth and Rembrandt of later times, who lived from 1746 to 1828, self-taught and full of defects, but fiery, original, masterly, and overflowing with tremendous power. He was an Aragonese by birth, and became court-painter to Charles IV. Between portraits of the nobles, pictures of the saints, and satires of the corrupt clergy, Goya's time was preciously occupied; yet he found opportunity to make many famous etchings, and to practise fresco-painting. He was the lone star in the long night of Spanish art.

Our glance at the later Spanish painters would not be thorough unless it included the noble names of Zamacois and Fortuny. The former still lives, and is performing illustrious work. Let us for a moment look at the picturesque life of the lamented Fortuny. He was a Catalonian by birth, and was educated at Barcelona. Afterwards he studied art at Rome, in the works of the old masters, and among the grand and desolate landscapes of the Campagna. During the war with Morocco he served as a staff-officer with Gen. Prim, and then returned to Rome and Florence, to illustrate the history of the last struggle of Spaniards with Moors in a painting of the

Battle of Tetuan, thirty feet long. He went to Paris in 1866; and his compatriot Zamacois introduced him to Mr. A. T. Stewart of New York, who gave him several rich commissions. Returning to Madrid, he married the daughter of Señor Madrazo, the director of the Museum; and painted several brilliant Arabic and Moorish scenes. In 1869 he was again in Paris; but on the outbreak of the Franco-German war he retired to Granada, where he occupied one of the old Saracenic palaces. In 1872 he went to Rome to take up his permanent abode, and hired a villa there; but the malaria soon poisoned him, and he died in 1874, after a short but wasting sickness. Fortuny was not a Spanish artist in the sense that Goya was, for Italy and Paris had exerted a profound influence upon his manner of thought and execution. Still in his Moorish scenes he sometimes approached the naturalistic style of his predecessors, under the outward forms of the French school. How far might he have gone towards Murillo if the face of the world had not so changed since the days of Pacheco? In our days the dogma of the Immaculate Conception has been made an article of faith, but it has not found reverent artists to portray its glories. The flying artillery of battle-pieces, the pretty poses of fair ladies of France, the solemn landscapes of the brumal North, have replaced on the painters' easels the ecstatic saints and seraphic Madonnas of the Age of Faith. The ancients appropriated the term *naturalistas* to designate the artists who dealt with the most unnatural and almost unimaginable of subjects; but it belongs more certainly to the masters of to-day, who illustrate the life of the bivouac, the street, and the fields. Murillo and Fortuny were the Spaniards of contrasted centuries, — the seventeenth, with its supreme Inquisition and its world-exploring *conquistadores*, — and the nineteenth, with its expanding liberalism and scientific analysis, shadowed as yet by cannon-smoke.

A LIST OF

THE PAINTINGS OF MURILLO

NOW IN EXISTENCE,

WITH THE DATES OF THEIR EXECUTION, AND THEIR PRESENT LOCATIONS.

₊ *The interrogation-point annexed to a title signifies that some critics consider the picture to be of doubtful authenticity.*

SPAIN.

MADRID. — *Museum*, — Holy Family (El Pajarito); Rebecca and Eliezer; Annunciation; Magdalen; St. Jerome; Adoration of the Shepherds; The Vision of St. Augustine; La Porciuncula, 1674–76; Virgin and Child; St. James; The Child Christ; St. John the Baptist as a Child; Jesus and St. John the Baptist as Children; The Annunciation; The Vision of St. Bernard; St. Ildefonso Receiving the Miraculous Chasuble; La Virgen del Rosario; The Conversion of St. Paul; St. Anna Teaching the Virgin Mary to

Read, 1675; Sketch for the preceding, 1675; The Crucifixion; St. Fernando, 1671; The Immaculate Conception, 1671; The Crucifixion; The Immaculate Conception; The Martyrdom of St. Andrew; The Child Christ Sleeping on the Cross; The Immaculate Conception; Four Scenes from the Life of the Prodigal Son, 1670-74; Head of St. John the Baptist; Head of St. Paul; St. Jerome Reading; St. Francis di Paola; The Old Spinster; Las Gallegas; St. Francis di Paola; Ecce Homo; two Landscapes; Portrait of Father Cabanillas; Our Lady of Sorrows.

MADRID. — *Academy of St. Fernando,* — El Tiñoso, 1670-74; two Pictures illustrating the Legend of Our Lady of the Snow, 1656; The Resurrection. *Marquis of Javalquinto,* — Portrait of Moreto. *Marquis of Salamanca,* — The Old Woman of Triana. *Duke of Uceda,* — The Child Christ Sleeping on the Cross; St. Rosalia. *Duke of Medina Cœli,* — Portrait. *Convent of the Angel Guardian,* — The Good Shepherd.

SEVILLE. — *Museum,* — The Nativity, 1674-77; The Adoration of the Shepherds, 1676; The Annunciation, 1674-77; The Madonna and the Dead Christ, 1674-77; St. Francis Embracing the Dead Christ; St. John in the Desert; St. Joseph and the Infant Christ, 1674-77; The Virgin of the Napkin, 1674-77; St. Felix; St. Augustine, 1678; The Immaculate Conception, 1674-77; The Virgin and St. Augustine, 1678; The Immaculate Conception; An Angel Holding the Hand of the Dead Christ; St. Leander and St. Bonaventura, 1674-77; St. Thomas of Villanueva, 1674-77; St. Anthony of Padua, 1674-77; The Vision of

St. Felix of Cantalicio; St. Justa and St. Rufina, 1676; The Virgin and San Pedro Nolasco; three more Immaculate Conceptions; The Crucifixion, early; The Vision of St. Anthony.

SEVILLE. — *Cathedral*, — St. Leander, 1655; St. Isidore, 1655; The Baptism of Christ, 1656; Ecce Homo; Madonna; The Immaculate Conception; eight Oval Paintings in the Chapter-house, 1668; St. Anthony of Padua, 1656; The Guardian Angel, 1674-77; The Abbess Dorotea de Villalda, 1674; St. Ferdinand; St. Ferdinand (in the Library). *La Caridad*, — The Miracle of the Loaves and Fishes, 1670-74; Moses Striking the Rock, 1670-74; The Infant St. John the Baptist; The Infant Christ; The Annunciation; The Charity of San Juan de Dios, 1670-74. *Santa Maria la Blanca*, — The Last Supper, early. *Marquis of Cessera*, — Painted Crucifix; Christ Bound. *Santelmo Palace*, — The Madonna de la Faja. *Late Pereira Collection*, — Madonna and St. Francis, before 1642; Madonna, Monk, and Angels, early.

VALLADOLID. — *Museum*, — St. Joseph and the Infant Christ.

CADIZ. — *Museum*, — Espousals of St. Catharine, 1682. *St. Felipe Neri*, — The Immaculate Conception. *Hospital*, — St. Francis Receiving the Stigmata; St. Francis di Paola Praying.

Stirling's list (1648) gives the following additional titles, many of which probably remain as then: MADRID. — *Madrazo Collection*, — Two Cherubs; Job and his Wife; The Virgin of the Rosary; St. Joseph's Dream; The Crucifixion; two Nuns.

XERES DE LA FRONTERA. — A Girl Paying Boy for Fruit.

SEVILLE. — *La Caridad,* — Tobit Burying the Strangled Man. *Don Julian Williams,* — The Immaculate Conception; Holy Family; Conversion of St. Paul; a Boy, like Cupid. *Juan Govantes,* — St. Augustine Writing; Father Villavizinas; two Angels Adoring the Mystical Lamb; Christ and John the Baptist as Children. *J. M. Escazena,* — Our Lady of Sorrows and St. John the Evangelist; Madonna and Child with the Infant St. John; Monk's Head; St. Anthony of Padua. *Capuchin Church,* — The Crucifixion.

ENGLAND.

LONDON. — *National Gallery,* — The Holy Family ("The Pedroso Murillo"); St. John and the Lamb; A Peasant-Boy.

Stafford House, — St. Justa; St. Rufina; Abraham Receiving the Three Angels, 1670–74; St. Anthony of Padua and the Infant Christ; the Return of the Prodigal Son, 1670–74; The Holy Family; A Girl with Fruit; Sts. Justa and Rufina; Portrait of a Gentleman; three small studies. *The Earl of Clarendon,* — The Head of St. John the Baptist; The Child Christ Sleeping; St. Athanasius. *George Tomline's Collection, Carlton Terrace,* — Christ Healing the Paralytic at the Pool of Bethesda, 1670–74; St. Augustine at Prayer; St. Joseph and Christ. *Grosvenor House (Marquis of Westminster),* — St. John and the Lamb; The Infant Christ Sleeping; Laban Hunting for his Gods in the Tent of Rachel.

LONDON. — *S. J. Lloyd,* — Madonna; Madonna Standing; The Immaculate Conception. *Dorchester House* (R S. Holford), — A Girl in a White Mantilla. *Col. H. Baill*' — The Immaculate Conception; The Madonna; A Knight of Santiago, The Madonna. *Right Hon. E. Ellice,* — The Madonna of the Rosary. *R. Sanderson,* — The Immaculate Conception; Portrait of a Lady. *Lansdowne House* (Marquis of Lansdowne), — The Immaculate Conception; The Virgin Kneeling.

H. A. J. Munro, — Miracle of the Loaves and Fishes; Deposition from the Cross; St. Peter Delivered from Prison; St. Anthony of Padua and the Infant Christ.

Apsley House (Duke of Wellington), — A Female Saint; St. Francis in Prayer; Isaac Blessing Jacob. *Col. Birchell,* — Ecce Homo. *Earl of Ellesmere,* — Lazarus and Dives. *T. Purvis,* — Apostle and Lad with Two Fishes; John the Baptist Questioned by the Jews; St. Peter the Dominican.

Earl Dudley, — Gypsy Woman, Boy, and Dog; St. Justa; The Virgin Covering the Body of St. Clara; St. John and the Lamb; six scenes from the Parable of the Prodigal Son. *Baron de Rothschild,* — The Good Shepherd; Christ as a Child. *Capt. W. C. Tupper,* — The Assumption. *F. Cooke,* — Ecce Homo. *R. W. Billings,* — La Virgen de la Faja. *Bath House,* — Boyhood of St. Thomas Villanueva. *R. Buchanan,* — Ecstasy of St. Giles 1646.

Late Northwick Collection, — Madonna; The Holy Family; Jacob and Laban's Cattle. *Late Brackenbury Collection,* — The Immaculate Conception; The Assumption; St.

Ferdinand with his Robe and Crown; The Immaculate Conception; St. Rosa of Lima and the Infant Christ. *Late Ashburton Collection*, — The Immaculate Conception; The Virgin, Christ, and John; Ecce Homo; St. Thomas of Villanueva; sketch for the preceding; Ecce Homo.

Leigh Court, Somerset (W. Miles), — The Annunciation; The Repose in Egypt; The Holy Family; Head of John the Baptist in a Charger; Deposition from the Cross; Martyrdom of St. Sebastian; St. John Writing the Apocalypse; Crucifixion of St. Andrew; Holy Family and Kneeling Prelate. *Stratton Park, Hants* (Sir F. Baring), — The Immaculate Conception; Holy Family; Shepherd Boy; The Ascension; Holy Family. *Blenheim Palace* (Duke of Marlborough), — Two Beggar-Boys. *W. Coningham, Bristol*, — Ivy-Crowned Boy. *Ockham, Surrey* (Earl of Lovelace), — St. John with the Lamb. *J. Cave, Bristol*, — Joseph and his Brethren. *Longford Castle, Wilts* (Earl of Radnor), — Ruth and Naomi. *Woburn Abbey* (Duke of Bedford), — Cherubs Gathering Flowers; Madonna and Child. *Kingston Hall, Dorset* (G. Banckes), — Angel with a Cardinal's Cap; St. Rosa of Lima and the Infant Christ; Two Boys Eating Fruit; An Angel.

Burleigh Hall, Northamptonshire (Marquis of Exeter), — The Beggar's Feast; Diogenes (?) Throwing Away his Cup.

Heytesbury House, Wilts, — St. John the Baptist; The Holy Family; A Woman and Girl. *Claverton Manor, Somerset* (George Vivian), — The Immaculate Conception; St. John the Baptist; Christ in the Clouds. *Windleston*

Hall, Durham (Sir W. Eden), — La Virgen de la Manzana The Madonna of the Rosary; The Virgin Appearing to St. Francis.

Dulwich College, — Flower-Girl; Two Gipsy Boys; Christ and the Lamb; The Immaculate Conception; Peasant Boys; Jacob and Rachel; The Adoration of the Magi; Two Angels; The Sleeping Child; The Immaculate Conception; The Crucifixion of St. Peter (?); Christ Bearing the Cross (?). *Hampton-Court Palace,* — Spanish Boy; Boy Eating Fruit; Don Carlos. *Lister House, Clapham* (George Field), — St. John the Baptist with a Lamb. *Oxford,* — St. John Questioned by the Jews.

Bowood, Wilts (Marquis of Lansdowne), — Christ Sleeping, as a Child; Don Justino Neve y Yevenes; Don Miguel Mañara. *D. Burdon, Newcastle-on-Tyne,* — The Baptism of Christ. *Tottenham Park, Wilts* (Earl of Ailesbury), — Christ and Mary at the Marriage-Feast of Cana. *Hevitre, Devon* (Richard Ford), — A Franciscan Praying; two drawings and an etching. *Lowther Castle* (Earl of Lonsdale), — A Boy Herding Cattle; Two Boys Eating Fruit. *Aston Hall, Cheshire* (Sir A. Aston), — Madonna; Portrait of Don Andres de Andrade. *Belvoir Castle, Leicestershire* (Duke of Rutland), — Madonna and Saints; Holy Family and St John; The Adoration of the Magi. *Chatsworth* (Duke of Devonshire), — The Holy Family.

The preceding list of Murillos in Great Britain is compiled from Mr. W. B. Scott's recent catalogue. Dr. Waagen enumerates the following in addition: *Wynn-Ellis Collection.* — St. Joseph and the Infant Christ; The Annunciation; two Shepherd-Girls. *Miss Rogers,* — The Infant Christ and St. Anthony of Padua. *G. A. Hoskins,* — St. Joseph and Christ; St. Thomas and Christ. *Holford Collection,* — The Virgin Praying; Head of the Madonna. *Marquis of Hertford,* — St. Thomas of Villanueva; The Conception, The Annunciation; The Ascension. *Glendor Hall,* — Spanish Boy. *Sir H. L. Bulwer,* — St. Bonaventura Writing his Memoirs After his Death. *Earl Listowell,* — The Espousals of Mary; Madonna; Birth of St. John. *Petworth,* — Monks Discoursing. *Charlton Park,* — Ascension of the Virgin; Coronation of the Virgin. *Wardour Castle,* — Joseph Relating his Dream. *Stourhead House,* — An Old Woman. *Warwick Castle,* — A Laughing Boy.

SCOTLAND.

Gosford House, East Lothian (Earl of Wemyss), — The Flight into Egypt; The Good Shepherd. *Broom Hall, Fifeshire* (Earl of Elgin), — St. John the Baptist; A Boy Eating Pie. *Glasgow University,* — The Good Shepherd. *H. A. J. Munro, Novar,* — Woman and Girl. *Sir W. Stirling-Maxwell, Keir,* Perthshire, — The Crucifixion; A Basket of Fruit. *Balbirnie, Fifeshire* (John Balfour), — Two Boys Eating Fruit. *Hamilton Palace,* — St. John the Baptist as a Child.

FRANCE.

PARIS. — *The Louvre,* — St. Thomas of Villanueva; The Immaculate Conception; St. Diego of Alcalá; Beggar-Boy; The Adoration of the Magi; The Nativity; Madonna and Child; Murillo; Anna de Salcedo; Don Andreas de Andrade; 22 drawings. MARSEILLES. — *Museum,* — A Capuchin.

ITALY.

ROME. — *Vatican,* — The Prodigal's Return; The Espousals of St. Catherine; The Adoration of the Shepherds. *Corsini Palace,* — Madonna. *Braschi Palace,* — Madonna and Angels. *Bracciano Palace,* — Mary Magdalene. *Doria Palace,* — Female Figure.

TURIN. — *Academy,* — A Capuchin; A Boy. MILAN. — *Brera,* — An Old Woman. MODENA. — *Museum,* — A Benedictine. FLORENCE. — *Pitti Palace,* — Two Madonnas.

GERMANY.

BERLIN, — A Cardinal; St. Anthony of Padua. DRESDEN, — Madonna and Child; Girl and Fruit. MUNICH, — *Pinakothek,* — St. Francis Healing a Cripple; Two Boys Eating Fruit; Four Boys Playing Cards; Two Boys Eating Bread and Fruit; Two Boys Playing Dice; Old Woman and Boy; Girl Paying a Boy for Fruit.

AUSTRIA.

VIENNA. — *The Belvedere,* — St. John the Baptist as a Child. PESTH (former Esterhazy Gallery), — Madonna and Child; Man with a Spade; St. Joseph and the Saviour; Holy Family.

NORTHERN EUROPE.

THE HAGUE, — The Immaculate Conception; Madonna and Child; St. John of the Cross. AMSTERDAM, — The Annunciation. ANTWERP, — Two Pictures of St. Francis STOCKHOLM, — Boys with a Basket.

RUSSIA.

St. Petersburg. — *The Hermitage Palace,* — Isaac Blessing Jacob; Jacob's Dream; The Annunciation, The Assumption; St. Joseph and the Saviour; The Flight into Egypt; The Holy Family; The Nativity; The Adoration of the Shepherds; St. Joseph and the Saviour; The Crucifixion; The Martyrdom of St. Peter the Dominican; The Flight into Egypt; Boy and Dog; Girl and Fruit; Portrait of a Gentleman; A Landscape; Sts. Florian, Dominic, and Peter the Dominican; and ten others.

INDEX.

Abraham and the Angels, 75.
Academy of Art, 55.
Aguado Collection, 117.
Alcazar, The, 24.
America, 14, 16.
Amiability of Murillo, 10, 65.
Ancient English Artists, 54.
Andalusia, 25.
Andalusian Art, 101.
Ariás, 18.
Austere Art, 53.

Beggar-boys, Murillo's, 106.
Betrothal of St. Catharine, 95.
Bodegones, 10.

Cadiz, 22, 96.
Cálido Manner, 35.
Cano, Alonso, 9, 18.
Capuchins, 79.
Caridad, La, 68.
Castillo, 9, 11, 40, 61.
Cathedral of Seville, 24, 38.
Caxes, 18.
Charity of San Juan, 73,
Children of the Shell, 88.
Collantes, 18.
Collections, 116.
Contemporaries, 23.
Contemporary Fame, 115.

Death of St. Clara, 29.
Death of Murillo, 99.
Descent from the Cross, 95, 99.
Doña Beatriz, 33.
Don Justino Neve, 40, 92, 93, 99.

Family of Murillo, 7.
Farfan's Eulogy, 59.
Feria, The, 12.
First Madonnas, 11.

Flemish Art, 15, 19.
Fortuny, 122.
Franciscan Pictures, 27.
French Plunderings, 30, 41, 60, 71, 93, 99, 113.
Frio Style, 32.

Gallegas, Las, 105.
Genre-Painting, 105.
Giralda, La, 24.
Gomez, Sebastian, 58.
Goya, 121.
Guardian Angel, The, 85.

Healing of the Paralytic, 76.
Herrera el Mozo, 42, 55, 57.
Herrera el Viejo, 10.
Home of Murillo, 62.

Image-Worship, 52.
Immaculate Conception, The, 44, 36, 41, 59, 60, 84, 93, 118.
Inquisition, The, 46, 80.
Invitation to Court, 60.
Iriarte, 86, 87.
Italian Studies, 14, 17, 19.

Jacob, Life of, 86.
Joanes, 54.
Journey to Madrid, 16.

Landscape-Painting, 109.
Latin Revival, 26.
Leonardo, 18.
Linage, Don, 64.
Lonja, The, 25.
Love at Pilas, 33.

Madonnas, The, 103.
Madrid, Life at, 16-21.
Mañara, 68, 94.

135

INDEX.

Market-Sales, 14.
Marriage, The, 33.
Mayno, 18.
Miracle of the Loaves and Fishes, 72.
Misty Manner, The, 41.
Moses Striking the Rock, 71.
Moya, 9, 15, 18.
Murillo, Francisca, 92.
—— Gabriel, 65.
—— Gaspar, 65, 99.
—— Teresa, 64.

Nails of the Cross, 50.
Napkin, Virgin of the, 82.
Nativity, The, 84.

Olivarez, 19, 20, 61.
Omazurino, 87.
Our Lady of the Snow, 40.

Pacheco, 10, 31, 37, 46.
Pecuniary Position, 63.
Pereda, 18.
Philip IV., 22.
Piety of Murillo, 66.
Popular Homage, 31.
Porciuncula, La, 80.
Portrait-Painting, 108.
Portraits of Murillo, 32, 62.
Prayerful Life, The, 67, 95.
Prodigal's Return, The, 75.

Rebecca and Eliezer, 88.
Release of St. Peter, The, 77.
Religious Painting, 102.
Repentance of St. Peter, 93.
Return to Seville, 21.
Ribera, 20.
Roelas, 10.

Rules for Painting, 47.
St. Anna and the Virgin, 49, 91.
St. Anthony of Padua, 38, 83.
St. Augustine, 94.
St. Bernard of Clairvaux, 90.
St. Diego of Alcalá, 28.
St. Elizabeth of Hungary, 74.
St. Francis, 28, 83.
St. George's Church, 70, 94.
St. Giles, 30.
St. Hermengild, 60.
St. Ildefonso, 89.
St. Isidore, 37.
Sts. *Justa and Rufina,* 59, 81.
St. Leander, 37, 81.
St. Thomas of Villanueva, 83.
School-days, 8.
Seville, 9, 24.
Social Position, 34.
Soult, Marshal, 30, 114.
Spain's Decadence, 22.
Spanish Art, 52, 112.
Spanish Isolation, 112.
Statue of Murillo, 100.
Studio, The, 63.

Tiñoso, El, 74.

Valbuena, 58.
Valdés Leal, 55, 57.
Van Dyck, 15, 20.
Vaporoso Style, 41.
Vargas, Luis de, 54.
Velazquez, 10, 17, 19, 20, 31, 65, 109, 118.
Vision of St. Felix, 84.

Will, Murillo's, 96.

Zurbaran, 18.

ALLSTON

PREFACE.

WASHINGTON ALLSTON was one of the highest products of American civilization and European culture combined, and possessed the full affluence of literary genius, artistic knowledge, refinement, purity, and religion as few other men of the Western World ever have. He was the intimate friend of Sumner and Irving, Coleridge and Wordsworth, Thorwaldsen and West, Longfellow and Channing, and many others of the foremost men of his age; and on all occasions proved himself worthy of their companionship, and even of their love.

Some materials for this biography were obtained from the memoirs of Leslie, Morse, Collins, Harding, Sumner, and other contemporaries of the artist; and from the writings of Tuckerman, Ware, and Dunlap. I have also examined nearly all the English memoirs and miscellanies relating to the first quarter of the nineteenth century, finding here and there chance allusions or original characterizations of my subject. But a large part of the facts herein set forth have been collected from the friends of Allston; and in this connection I would hereby render my thanks to Mr. Richard H. Dana, Jr., and other members of the Dana family, and also to Messrs. Jonathan Mason, George S. Hillard, Henry W. Longfellow, Robert C. Winthrop, Robert C. Waterston, and other New-England gentlemen who have given me facts about Allston's life. I would also gratefully acknowledge similar assistance from Messrs. Daniel Ravenel and S. P. Ravenel of Charleston, S. C.; the Rev. Benjamin Allston, of Georgetown, S. C.; Captain Joseph Blyth Allston, of Baltimore; and other members of the Allston family.

I have preferred to give as much of the autobiographical character as possible to this sketch, by using Allston's own words on all available occasions, and supplementing them with the language of Morse, Leslie, Collins, Sumner, Irving, Lowell, Felton, and Dana. In this way we may gain a clear and living idea of the great artist and his surroundings, as he appeared to his contemporaries and associates, and may, perchance, comprehend the secret of his fascination.

M. F. SWEETSER.

CONTENTS.

CHAPTER I.

Waccamaw. — The Allstons. — Childhood of the Master. — Newport. — Channing and Dana. — Harvard College. — Malbone. — Return to South Carolina. — Youth's Joys 7

CHAPTER II.

Studies in London. — West, Fuseli, and Northcote. — With Vanderlyn at Paris. — Switzerland and the Italian Lakes. — Rome. — Thorwaldsen and the Humboldts. — Irving and Coleridge. — "The American Titian." — Return to America. — Marriage to Miss Channing 31

CHAPTER III.

Return to London. — Collins, Leslie, and Morse. — Sir George Beaumont. — West. — Coleridge and Southey. — Death of Mrs. Allston. — Paris. — Lord Egremont. — Irving. — Homeward Bound 55

CHAPTER IV.

The Studio at Boston. — Chester Harding. — Academic Honors. — Horatio Greenough. — Washington Irving. — De Veaux. — Morse 92

CHAPTER V.

A Group of Pictures. — The Valentine, Rosalie, Beatrice, Spalatro, etc. — The 'Belshazzar's Feast' 109

CHAPTER VI.

The Studio at Cambridgeport. — Lowell's Pen-Sketch. — Mrs. Jameson. — The Exhibition. — Eminent Friends. — The Death of Allston 131

CHAPTER VII.

Allston as an Author. — "The Sylphs." — "The Two Painters." — Minor Poems. — "Monaldi." — "Lectures on Art." — Studio Aphorisms 156

CHAPTER VIII.

Personal Traits. — System of Color. — Versatility. — Italianism. — Slight Influence on American Art 172

ALLSTON.

CHAPTER I.

Waccamaw. — The Allstons. — Childhood of the Master. — Newport. — Channing and Dana. — Harvard College. — Malbone. — Return to South Carolina. — Youth's Joys.

THE district of Waccamaw, in South Carolina, is a long strip of land, between the Waccamaw River and the Ocean, from three to six miles wide, and separated by Winyah Bay, on the south, from the Santee country. On this sequestered and sea-fronting peninsula, a century ago, several patrician families lived under an almost baronial *régime*, with their broad plantations, their many vassals, and their generous hospitalities. Prominent among these were the Allstons, from whom arose one of the foremost of American artists.

It is supposed that the Allstons came from the Norse settlements in Northumberland, and from a baronet's family. There is a town in that county by the name of Alston, and one in Norway called Alsten. Some people think that the American Allstons were descended from John Allston, who was banished from England about the year 1685, for complicity in the rebellion of the Duke of Monmouth.

William Allston of Brook Green was the nephew of Colonel William Allston, of Marion's staff, who married the daughter of the heroic Rebecca Motte. The younger William had two children, Benjamin and Elizabeth, by his first wife; and three by his second wife, Mary, WASHINGTON, and William Moore Allston. Benjamin was therefore Washington's half-brother, and his son was Governor R. F. W. Allston, whose son Benjamin, a retired army officer, now resides in the Waccamaw region. Mr. Joseph B. Allston, of Baltimore, and late of the Confederate army, a gentleman famous for his ringing war-poetry, is another grand-nephew of our artist.

Governor Joseph Allston, of South Carolina, who married Theodosia, the daughter of Aaron Burr, was the son of the painter's great-uncle, Colonel William Allston; and his brother, William

Algernon Allston, married Mary Allston, the sister of Washington. The artist's younger brother, William, studied at Princeton College, and settled in the North, where he married a Miss Rogers, by whom he had three children.

William Allston had several estates in the Waccamaw region, and chose the Springfield plantation as Washington's heritage, while Brook Green was allotted to Benjamin. In the year 1780, before his son Washington had attained his second birthday, William died; and Mrs. Rachel Allston afterwards married Dr. Henry C. Flagg, of Rhode Island, an officer of the Continental army.

We cannot better describe the Allston mansions and their people, a century ago, than in the words of General Horry, one of Marion's partisan officers: "These three spirited charges, having cost us a great deal of rapid marching and fatigue, Marion said he would give us '*a little rest.*' So he led us down into Waccamaw, where he knew we had some excellent friends; among whom were the Hugers and Trapiers, and the Allstons; fine fellows! rich as Jews, and *hearty* as we could wish: indeed, the worthy

Captain, now Colonel, William Allston, was one of Marion's aids. These great people all received us as though we had been their brothers, threw open the gates of their elegant yards for our cavalry, hurried us up their princely steps; and, notwithstanding our dirt and rags, ushered us into their grand saloons and dining-rooms, where the famous mahogany sideboards were quickly covered with pitchers of old amber-colored brandy, and sugar dishes of *double refined*, with honey, for drams and juleps. Our horses were up to the eyes in corn and sweet-scented fodder; while, as to ourselves, nothing that air, land, or water could furnish was good enough for us. Fish, flesh, and fowl, all of the *fattest and finest*, and sweetly graced with the smiles of the great ladies, were spread before us as though we had been kings; while Congress and Washington went round in sparkling bumpers, from old demijohns that had not left the garret for many a year. This was feasting indeed!"

On the Brook Green domain, twenty-two miles above Georgetown, in the mansion-house of his family, Washington Allston was born, on the fifth of November, 1779. The house in which he came into life has since been destroyed. From his earliest years he was distinguished by a nervous and active temperament, a quick mind, and an acute sensibility, conditions peculiarly unfavorable to his development in the languid atmosphere of the Carolinas, and under the dull routine of a plantation-home.

Allston has thus written of his early years, and of the first manifestations of his genius for composition and landscape, and love for the marvellous and poetic: —

"To go back as far as I can, — I remember that I used to draw before I left Carolina, at six years of age (by the way, no *uncommon* thing), and still earlier, that my favorite amusement, much akin to it, was making little landscapes about the roots of an old tree in the country, — meagre enough, no doubt, — the only particulars of which I can call to mind were a cottage built of sticks, shaded by little trees, which were composed of the small suckers (I think so called), resembling miniature trees, which I gathered in the woods. Another employment was the converting the forked stalks of the wild ferns into little men and women, by winding about them different colored yarn. These were sometimes presented with pitchers made of the pomegranate flower. These childish fancies were the straws by which, perhaps, an observer might then have guessed which way the current was setting for after life. And yet, after all, this love of imitation may be common to childhood. General imitation certainly is; but whether adherence to particular kinds may not indicate a permanent propensity, I leave to those who have studied the subject more than I have, to decide.

"But even these delights would sometimes give way to a stronger love for the wild and marvellous. I delighted in being terrified by the tales of witches and hags, which the negroes used to tell me; and I well remember with what pleasure I recalled these feelings on my return to Carolina, especially on revisiting a gigantic wild grape-vine in the woods, which had been the favorite swing for one of these witches.

"One of my favorite haunts when a child in Carolina was a forest spring, where I used to catch minnows, and, I dare say, with all the callousness of a fisherman; at this moment I can see that spring, and the pleasant conjurer Memory has brought again those little creatures before me; but how unlike to what they were! They seem to me like the spirits of the woods, which a flash from their little diamond eyes lights up afresh in all their gorgeous garniture of leaves and flowers."

When the boy had reached his seventh year the family physician advised that he should be sent to the North, in order that his nervous and high-strung organization might be recruited by a more bracing air than that of the Carolina lowlands. The education befitting the son of a Southern planter could hardly be obtained on a secluded estate like that of the Allstons, and the desire to place their heir in a situation favorable to his intellectual culture was another reason why his parents resolved to send him away for a few years. In those days there was but one place for a Carolina lad to be educated in, and that was Newport, R. I., whither young Washington was sent.

The excellent schools of Newport afforded facilities for the proper education of the Southern children, many of whom were left here to be prepared for college. John C. Calhoun received his elementary tuition here, before going to Yale College. James Hamilton was educated here, and afterwards reversed his Northern indoctrination by forcing South Carolina into conflict with the United States, and advocating the Nullification Act, while he was governor. The Kinlocks of Charleston were summer visitors at Newport from 1785 to 1800, and other Carolinians there were the Shubricks, Rutledges, Gists, and Hayneses. The Carolina colony at Newport flourished and increased until it was ruined by the fatal results of the Rutledge-Senter duel.

The connection between Newport and Allston's parish was always peculiarly intimate. An Allston was born in Rhode Island, and appointed thence to West Point in 1820. At the reunion of the Sons of Newport, in 1859, there were seven old Rhode-Islanders present from Georgetown, S. C., the town nearest to the Allston estates.

From 1785 to 1800 Newport was one of the most cultivated and wealthy communities of the United States, the chief naval station of the Republic, and hardly second to New York in commerce. The wealth acquired by maritime trading had given opportunity for the development of numerous aristocratic families, with whom social life and elegant hospitalities had been refined by the visits of distinguished foreigners and the frequent sojourns of the courtly officers of the French fleets, whose favorite rendezvous during the Revolutionary war had been in this harbor. There was also less of ecclesiastical intolerance here than among the Puritan colonies on the north and west, and a superior ease and freedom of life and manners. The intellectual stimulus which Dean Berkeley had given to the society of the town in 1729 – 31 had been aided by the foundation of the Redwood Library a few years later, and resulted in a notable degree of scholarship and culture. Dr. Waterhouse of Harvard University stated that the laboratories of Newport were then the best in America. Nor was art so nearly unknown here as in the other small American towns, for Smybert had accompanied Berkeley in his sojourn on these shores, and portrayed several of the Rhode-Islanders. Blackburn had visited Newport on the same errand, as early as 1754; and Cosmo Alexander painted here in 1770. Robert Feke was a skilful local artist; Gilbert Stuart obtained his education in Newport, and began to paint here; and Malbone was a native of the town and a scion of one of its best families. As early as 1730, Henry Collins, a wealthy merchant of this place, had collected a notable gallery of paintings, including portraits which he caused Smybert to paint of Dean Berkeley, Callender, Hitchcock, and Clapp.

The master thus speaks of his boyhood at Newport: "My chief pleasure now was in drawing from prints, — of all kinds of figures, landscape, and animals. But I soon began to make pictures of my own; at what age, however, I cannot say. The earliest compositions that I remember were the storming of Count Roderick's castle, from a poor (though to me delightful) romance of that day, and the siege of Toulon; the first in Indian-ink, the other in water-colors. I cannot recall the year in which they were done. To these succeeded many others, which have likewise passed into oblivion. Though I never had any regular instructor in the art (a circumstance, I would here observe, both idle and absurd to boast of), I had much incidental instruction, which I have always through life been glad to receive from every one in advance of myself. And, I may add, there is no such thing as a self-taught artist, in the ignorant acceptation of the word ; for the greatest genius that ever lived must be indebted to others, if not by direct teaching, at least indirectly through their works. I had, in my school-days, some of this latter kind of instruction from a very worthy and amiable man, a Mr. King, of Newport, who made quadrants and compasses, and occasionally painted portraits. I believe he was originally bred a painter, but obliged, from the rare calls upon his pencil, to call in the aid of another craft. I used at first to make frequent excuses for visiting his shop to look at his pictures, but finding that he always received me kindly, I went at last without any, or rather with the avowed purpose of making him a visit. Sometimes I would take with me a drawing, and was sure to get a kind word of encouragement. It was a pleasant thing to me, some twenty years after this, to remind the old man of these little kindnesses."

This was not the only recompense which Allston made to his generous old friend, for one of his first oil-paintings was a portrait of Mr. King, bearing a distinct prophecy of the warm and mellow tone and rich coloring of the artist's later works. The face is filled with a pleasing benignity, and the head has a noble and striking contour.

While a boy, Allston was distinguished among his playmates for his quick and almost fiery spirit and for his indomitable courage. An interesting school-boy friendship sprung up between him and a young native of Newport, William Ellery Channing, and lasted for many decades, beautiful and unimpaired. Together these inspired lads rambled through the charming country around the town, and along the resounding shore of the beaches, receiving such impressions of the beautiful and the sublime as had a profound influence upon their after-lives. Fifty years later Allston described Channing as having been a generous and noble-minded boy, his leader and exemplar, though several months younger. Another companion in these walks was Channing's cousin, Richard H. Dana, who was a sensitive and high-strung child, younger than either of the others. The intimacy between these three was still kept up in the pale winter of their age, when the venerable artist, the saintly divine, and the manly poet were accustomed to visit each other frequently, in their quiet Boston homes.

Of his life at Harvard College he says: —

"My leisure hours at college were chiefly devoted to the pencil, to the composition equally of figures and landscapes; I do not remember that I preferred one to the other; my only guide in the choice was the inclination of the moment. There was an old landscape at the house of a friend in Cambridge (whether Italian or Spanish I know not) that gave me my first hints in color in that branch; it was of a rich and deep tone, though not by the hand of a master; the work, perhaps, of a moderate artist, but of one who lived in a *good age*, when he could not help catching some of the good that was abroad. In the coloring of figures, the pictures of Pine, in the Columbian Museum, in Boston, were my first masters. Pine had certainly, as far as I can recollect, considerable merit in color. But I had a higher master in the head of Cardinal Bentivoglio, from Van Dyck, in the college library, which I obtained permission to copy one winter vacation. This copy from Van Dyck was by Smybert, an English painter, who came to this country with Dean, afterwards Bishop, Berkeley. At that time it seemed to me perfection; but when I saw the original some years afterwards, I found I had to alter my notions of perfection. However, I am grateful to Smybert for the instruction he gave me, — his work rather. Deliver me from kicking down even the weakest step of an early ladder." (The same picture by Smybert had previously awakened the first artistic impulses in the soul of John Trumbull, whose skilful pencil afterwards depicted the great events of the Revolutionary era in America.)

"I became acquainted with Malbone but a short time before he quitted Newport, a circumstance which I remember then regretting exceedingly, for I looked up to him with great admiration. Our not meeting earlier was owing, I suppose, to his going to another school, and being some years older than myself. I recollect borrowing some of his pictures on oiled paper to copy. Our intimacy, however, did not begin till I entered college, when I found him established at Boston. He had then (for the interval was of several years) reached the maturity of his powers, and was deservedly ranked the first miniature-painter in the country. Malbone's merits as an artist are too well known to need setting forth by me: I shall therefore say but a few words on that head. He had the happy talent, among his many excellences, of elevating the character without impairing the likeness: this was remarkable in his male heads; and no woman ever lost any beauty from his hand; nay, the fair would often become still fairer under his pencil. To this he added a grace of execution all his own. My admiration of Malbone induced me at this time (in my Freshman year at college) to try my hand at miniature, but it was without success. I could *make no hand of it;* all my attempts in that line being so far inferior to what I could *then* do in oil, that I became disgusted with my abortive efforts, and gave it up. One of these miniatures, or rather attempts at miniature, was shown me several years after, and I pronounced it '*without promise,*' not knowing it to be my own. I may add, I would have said the same had I known it. I may observe, however (for I know not why I should not be as just to myself as to another person), that I should not have expressed a similar opinion respecting its contemporaries in oil; for a landscape with figures on horseback, painted about this time, was afterwards exhibited at Somerset House."

Forty years later he presented Mr. Waterston with a beautiful little sketch which he made in 1798. Three other early sketches, in pencil, now in the possession of Mr. R. H. Dana, represent log-huts and block-houses, and were probably copied from some book on rural architecture. Other drawings of this time are of romantic and tragic scenes, — a scene from Schiller's "Robbers," a castle from "The Mysteries of Udolpho," and that weird picture of a maniac crushing a dove, which Sully so much admired. A vein of contrasted sentiment appeared in the ludicrous caricatures with which he filled the blank leaves of his own and his classmates' text-books.

At this period Harvard had less than two hundred students, and was under the presidency of Dr. Joseph Willard. Massachusetts and Hollis Halls were the chief dormitories, and Harvard Hall contained the chapel, library, and dining-room. The most prosperous societies were the Institute of 1770, the Speaking Club, and the Phi Beta Kappa, all of which were literary; the Adelphi, a religious union; and the Porcellian and Hasty-Pudding Clubs, devoted to social mysteries and much debating. Allston belonged to the two last named, and one of the record-books of the latter (of which he was secretary) contains a pen-sketch by his hand, depicting a youth seated before a huge caldron, and ladling its contents into his mouth.

Dr. Waterhouse, the professor of medicine, held Allston under his special care while in college, and had a paternal friendship for him. He claims that the youth's first essay in oil-painting was a portrait of his eldest boy, which was in the doctor's possession as late as 1833.

It is said that Allston, before he went abroad, painted four portraits of members of the Channing family, including his firm friend William Ellery. William visited Allston almost daily while they were in college, and the latter once drew for him a quaint group of pyramidal figures, composed of mild caricatures of the professors and tutors, which Channing offered at his recitation on mensuration. During his Junior year he wrote to Allston, saying, "I have no inclination for either divinity, law, or physic."

A favorite resort of the young Carolinian was the mansion of Judge Francis Dana, the Chief Justice of Massachusetts, and ex-minister to Russia. This house was situated on Dana Hill, between Harvard University and Boston, and was surrounded by wide fields which pertained to the estate, and were afterwards laid out in streets and occupied by a large population. Judge Dana was one of the most hospitable of men, and frequently entertained the chiefs of the Federal party and the leading men of the State. His house was almost a home to many of the students at the college, especially those from the South and the Middle States. Allston was at that time passionately fond of society, and became a very frequent visitor at the Dana mansion.

Among his classmates were Joseph S. Buckminster, afterwards a celebrated Unitarian divine and scholar; Lemuel Shaw, a profound jurist, and Chief Justice of Massachusetts; Charles Lowell, D. D., another liberal theologian, the father of J. R. and R. T. S. Lowell; Joshua Bates, D. D.,

President of Middlebury College; and Timothy Flint, famous for his writings about the Mississippi Valley and the Far West.

Allston's genius for poetry manifested itself during his college years, and won high consideration for the young Southron. Harvard College voted to mourn the death of Washington, in December, 1799, by the following exercises: "An introductory Address in Latin by the President. An Elegiac Poem in English by Washington Allston, a Senior Sophister. A Funeral Oration by Benjamin Marston Watson, a Senior Sophister. A Solemn and Pathetic Discourse by the Hollis Professor of Divinity." Once more he appeared as a poet, on taking his degree.

As soon as his college career was over, Allston hastened south to Charleston, where Malbone had already established himself, and was meeting with great success. Charleston was in those days pre-eminent among the Southern cities in its encouragement of art, chiefly in the line of portraits of the members of the patrician Carolina families. Charles Fraser, a native of the city, painted no fewer than 313 miniatures and 139 landscapes and compositions, illustrating the fair country around Charleston, as well as the clear-cut features of the Hugers, Pettigrus, and Pinkneys. Sully had settled in the city late in the last century; Waldo of Connecticut was liberally patronized there by the Rutledges; De Veaux excelled in portraits of the planters; Coram was busy in Carolina about 1780; and Earle also practised there, in the manner of Benjamin West.

Allston humorously called his studio at Charleston a "picture-manufactory"; and its chief productions appear to have been a head of Judas Iscariot, and another of St. Peter when he heard the cock crow. The latter, together with some of the youth's college verses, aroused the keen interest of Mr. Bowman, a wealthy Carolinian of Scottish birth, who immediately sought out and generously befriended their author. Bowman was a ripe scholar and an accomplished conversationalist, and delighted to welcome Allston, Malbone, and Fraser to his frequent dinner-parties. In after years his memory was most dear to his *protégé*. About this time Malbone painted a beautiful miniature of the young artist, which is still preserved in Charleston.

The Allston estates at Waccamaw were in the

hands of executors, one of whom offered the young heir a fraction of its real value for his part of the property. The artist's heart was with the æsthetic treasures of Europe, and had no yearning for the patriarchal life of a Carolina planter; and so, fearful of litigation and delays, and unskilled in matters of business, he disposed of his share of the paternal domain at a ruinous sacrifice, and appropriated the proceeds to his support in Europe. Not only that, but so ignorant was he of affairs that he made no attempt to live on the generous interest which might have accrued from the moneys which he received, but deposited his funds with a London banker, and drew directly and freely thereon until they were exhausted.

Certain generous Carolinians, unwilling to have the Waccamaw plantation pass out of the Allston family, offered to advance funds for the youth to make his foreign sojourn with; but he declined these proposals, preferring to keep his independence and to learn to rely on himself. Mr. Bowman insisted on his accepting £100 a year from him during the journey and the period of studying; and when this was declined, he proposed to ship several tierces of rice for him. Refusing even this, and when Bowman would not let him go without a present, Allston accepted Hume's History of England and a novel by Dr. Moore, with a letter of introduction to the latter.

The master himself has thus described his morning years: "With youth, health, the kindest friends, and ever before me buoyant hope, what a time to look back upon! I cannot but think that the life of an artist, whether painter or poet, depends much on a happy youth; I do not mean as to outward circumstances, but as to his inward being; in my own case, at least, I feel the dependence; for I seldom step into the ideal world without I find myself going back to the age of first impressions. The germs of our best thoughts are certainly often to be found there; sometimes, indeed (though rarely), we find them in full flower; and when so, how beautiful seem to us these flowers through an atmosphere of thirty years! 'T is in this way that poets and painters keep their minds young. How else could an old man make the page or the canvas palpitate with the hopes, and fears, and joys, the impetuous, impassioned emotions of youthful lovers or reckless heroes? There is a period of life when the ocean of time seems to force upon the mind a barrier against itself, forming, as it were, a permanent beach, on which the advancing years successively break, only to be carried back by a returning current to that furthest deep whence they first flowed. Upon this beach the *poetry of life* may be said to have its birth; where the *real* ends and the *ideal* begins. . . .

" Up to this time my favorite subjects, with an occasional comic intermission, were banditti. I well remember one of these, where I thought I had happily succeeded in cutting a throat! The subject of this precious performance was, robbers fighting with each other for the spoils, over the body of a murdered traveller. And clever ruffians I thought them. I did not get rid of this banditti mania until I had been over a year in England. It seems that a fondness for violence is common with young artists. One might suppose that the youthful mind would delight in scenes of an opposite character. Perhaps the reason of the contrary may be found in this: that the natural condition of youth being one incessant excitement, from the continued influx of novelty, — for all about us must *at one time be new*, — it must needs have something fierce, terrible, or unusual to force it above its wonted tone. But the time must come to every man who lives beyond the middle age, when 'there is nothing new under the sun.' His novelties then are the *rifacimenti* of his former life. The gentler emotions are then as early friends who revisit him in dreams, and who, recalling the past, give a grace and beauty, nay, a rapture even, to what in the heyday of youth had seemed to him spiritless and flat. And how beautiful is this law of nature, — perfuming, as it were, our very graves with the unheeded flowers of childhood."

CHAPTER II.

Studies in London. — West, Fuseli, and Northcote. — With Vanderlyn at Paris. — Switzerland and the Italian Lakes. — Rome. — Thorwaldsen and the Humboldts. — Irving and Coleridge. — "The American Titian." — Return to America. — Marriage to Miss Channing.

In May, 1801, Allston embarked for England, in company with his congenial friend Malbone. The latter remained in London five months, studying the pictures there, and executing his exquisite masterpiece, 'The Hours' (now in the Providence Athenæum). He then returned to Charleston, and our artist never saw him again.

Soon after Allston's arrival in London he obtained permission to draw at the Royal Academy, by submitting a drawing from a cast of the Gladiator; and another sketch won for him the ticket of an entered student. "Mr. West received me with the greatest kindness, — I shall never forget his benevolent smile when he took me by the hand: it is still fresh in my memory, linked with the last of like kind which accompanied the last shake of his hand, when I took a final leave of him in 1818. His gallery was open to me at all times, and his advice always ready and kindly given. He was a man overflowing with the milk of human kindness." Allston was fascinated by the exquisite taste of Sir Joshua Reynolds's pictures, and expressed his wonder at the slight acquaintance which had existed between Reynolds, Gainsborough, and Wilson, three men who had emerged, with a common purpose, from an age of lead. He thought Fuseli the greatest of living painters (a belief which was afterwards qualified), and was made happy by a courteous welcome to the Swiss artist's studio. He told him that he had journeyed to London in the hope of becoming an historical painter, and was answered, drearily enough, "Then you have come *a great way* to starve, sir." Fuseli had recently exhibited a series of pictures in illustration of Milton, and showed Allston such of the canvases as were not rolled up, being highly pleased with the youth's enthusiastic praises and his free quotations from the great English poet.

The young student began his labors by drawing from plaster casts, at the Royal Academy. The huge paintings of West appear to have exercised no effect upon him, and it was not until after he returned to America that his true inclination appeared. The academic precision learned in London was cold and meaningless to his mind, until the magic wand of the Venetian coloring awakened him to the glory of a higher art.

Bowman's letter to the author of "Zeluco" was never delivered, for the gifted Moore died about the time of Allston's arrival in London. But the high culture and delightful conversation of the young Carolinian secured admission for him to the best literary and artistic circles of the city, and his subsequent reminiscences of metropolitan life were full of interest and attraction. He was also a great favorite among his professional brethren, to whom he was introduced and commended by the venerable West. But his numerous social engagements were not allowed to conflict with his studies, which he practised for more than two years with great assiduity.

About this time, also, Rembrandt Peale, of

Pennsylvania, entered West's studio as a pupil, and was introduced to Allston and Lawrence.

Our artist's habit at this period was to read one or two articles from Pilkington's Dictionary of Painters, as an accompaniment to his breakfast, before entering upon the labors of the day. Many of these were written by Fuseli, whom he regarded as an inspiring and graphic critic, giving clear ideas and a distinct apprehension of the works of many painters with whom he was altogether unfamiliar. Allston has preserved several sparkling anecdotes of Fuseli and his contemporaries, two of which we may give here. Sir William Beechy was criticising a young artist's picture, and said, "Very well, C., very well indeed. You have improved, C. But, C., why did you make the coat and the background of the same color?" "For harmony, sir," replied the youth. "O, no! C., that's not harmony, that's monotony." Again, Fuseli asked the opinion of the Academy porter on one of his new pictures. "Law! Mr. Fuseli, I don't know anything of pictures." "But you know a horse, Sam; you have been in the Guards, you can tell if that is like a horse?" "Yes, sir." "Well?"

"Why, it seems to me, then, Mr. Fuseli, that — that five men could ride on him." "Then you think his back too long?" "A bit, sir."

Allston was also acquainted with Northcote, the crusty old Devonshire painter, and pupil of Sir Joshua Reynolds. He used to tell that he once asked Northcote's opinion as to the merits of William Hamilton, one of the illustrators of Boydell's Shakespeare, and the tart answer was made, "A very silly painter, sir, a very silly painter." Of the pictures of Reynolds, Northcote's master, the young Carolinan thought so highly that he said, "There is a fascination about them which makes it almost *ungrateful* to think of their defects."

So fearless was Allston of his ability that he sent three pictures to the Exhibition of the Royal Academy, — 'A French Soldier telling a Story,' 'A Rocky Coast with Banditti,' and 'A Landscape with Horsemen.' The latter was painted while the artist was at Harvard; and the 'French Soldier' was sold to the European Museum, whose proprietor ordered a companion-picture, 'The Poet's Ordinary.' These two were comic subjects, and were perhaps accompanied by others of a similar character, for the biographer of Sir Thomas Lawrence makes the following amazing statement: "In mentioning American painters, it would be unpardonable to omit the broad humor, in the style of Hogarth, in the pictures by Mr. Allston." It is to be noticed that Holmes also finds the spirit of Hogarth in some of the artist's earlier sketches.

In November, 1803, Allston and Vanderlyn, the gifted and unfortunate American painter, journeyed from London to the Low Countries, and from thence to Paris. The former remained for several months in the French capital, and painted four pictures, besides copying one of Rubens's works, in the Luxembourg, and Paul Veronese's great composition of "The Marriage at Cana." He said that during his sojourn at Paris he "worked like a mechanic."

Never before nor since was there such a magnificent collection of pictures and statuary as that which dazzled the eyes of Paris at this time, attesting the victories of Napoleon by the choicest art-treasures of the Continent. The Louvre contained the noblest works of Raphael and Titian, from Italy; the masterpieces of Murillo, stolen from Spain; and the richest flowerings of Teutonic and Batavian art, which had been torn from the German and Flemish churches and palaces. Through this peerless gallery the poet-painter rambled for weeks, attended by Vanderlyn, a worthy comrade. He wrote thus: "Titian, Tintoret, and Paul Veronese absolutely enchanted me, for they took away all sense of subject. When I stood before the Peter Martyr, the Miracle of the Slave, and the Marriage at Cana, I thought of nothing but of the *gorgeous concert of colors*, or rather of the indefinite forms (I cannot call them sensations) of pleasure with which they filled the imagination. It was the poetry of color which I felt; procreative in its nature, giving birth to a thousand things which the eye cannot see, and distinct from their cause. I did not, however, stop to analyze my feelings, — perhaps at that time I could not have done it. I was content with my pleasure without seeking the cause. But I now understand it, and *think* I understand *why* so many great colorists, especially Tintoret and Paul Veronese, gave so little heed to the ostensible *stories* of their compositions. In some of them, the Marriage at Cana, for instance, there is not the slightest clew given by which the spectator can guess at the subject. They addressed themselves, not to the senses merely, as some have supposed, but rather through them to that region (if I may so speak) of the imagination which is supposed to be under the exclusive dominion of music, and which, by similar excitement, they caused to teem with visions that 'lap the soul in Elysium.' In other words, they leave the subject to be made by the spectator, provided he possesses the imaginative faculty, — otherwise they will have little more meaning to him than a calico counterpane."

After the sojourn at Paris (let us borrow the beautiful words of Charles Sumner), "he directed his steps toward Italy, the enchanted ground of literature, history, and art, — strown with richest memorials of the Past, — filled with scenes memorable in the Progress of Man, — teaching by the pages of philosophers and historians, — vocal with the melody of poets, — ringing with the music which St. Cecilia protects, — glowing with the living marble and canvas, — beneath a sky of heavenly purity and brightness, — with the sunsets which Claude has painted, — parted by the Apennines, early witnesses of the unrecorded Etruscan civilization; surrounded by the snow-capped Alps, and the blue, classic waters of the Mediterranean Sea. The deluge of war submerging Europe had subsided here, and our artist took up his peaceful abode in Rome, the modern home of Art."

On his way from Paris to Italy, Allston leisurely traversed Switzerland, and experienced the keenest pleasure from a contemplation of its grand scenery. He crossed the Lake of Lucerne, and then went over the St. Gotthard Pass to Bellinzona and the exquisite lakes of Northern Italy. He says: "The impressions left by the sublime scenery of Switzerland are still fresh to this day. A new world had been opened to me, — nor have I met with anything like it since. The scenery of the Apennines is quite of a different character. By the by, I was particularly struck in this journey with the truth of Turner's Swiss scenes, — the poetic truth, — which none before or since have given, with the exception of my friend Brokedon's magnificent work on the passes of the Alps. I passed a night, and saw the sun rise, on the Lake Maggiore. Such a sunrise! The giant Alps seemed literally to rise from their purple beds, and, putting on their crowns of gold, to send up a hallelujah almost audible."

Allston left London in November, 1803, and entered Rome in March, 1805, and there is nearly a year of this interval unaccounted for. It was doubtless during this period that he made a long visit to Florence, where he painted the picture which is now in the Boston Athenæum. Some part of the time was probably spent at Venice, in studying the processes of that school of art to which the American master afterwards clung so closely.

Late in 1805 Vanderlyn rejoined Allston in Rome, and these two were the only students from America then in the city. They cast in their lots with an association of youths from Germany, Sweden, and Denmark, who assembled frequently to draw from the living model; and although the two transatlantic students lacked the government patronage and pensions which so greatly aided their European rivals, they had marked success in contending for the honors of their art.

The four years which Allston spent in Italy

were devoted to an earnest study of the old masters, and of that oldest master, Nature, whose fairest works are lavishly displayed in the land of the Apennines, — between Ætna and the Alps. The effects of this long communion with such sources of inspiration appeared in his subsequent pictures and writings, and added a new charm to his graceful conversation. He was profoundly moved by the contemplation of the great masterpieces of art at Rome, and enjoyed them in a spirit sufficiently rare among youths of his age, saying, "I had rather see a picture which I could not equal than one which I could surpass." It was the same sentiment which he expressed, in after years, in the words, "I had rather be the second painter in the world than the first, because I could then have some one to admire and look up to."

Allston has himself told how he was moved by the masterpieces of ancient art. "It is needless to say how I was affected by Raphael, the greatest master of the affections in our art. In beauty he has often been surpassed, but in grace, — the native grace of character, — in the expression of intellect, and, above all, sanctity, he has no equal. What particularly struck me in his works was the *genuine* life (if I may so call it) that seemed, without impairing the distinctive character, to pervade them all; for even his humblest figures have a *something*, either in look, air, or gesture, akin to the *venustas* of his own nature, as if, like living beings under the influence of a master-spirit, they had partaken, in spite of themselves, of a portion of the charm which swayed them. This power of infusing one's *own life*, as it were, into that which is feigned, appears to me the sole prerogative of genius. In a work of art, this is what a man may well call *his own;* for it cannot be borrowed or imitated. Of Michael Angelo I know not how to speak in adequate terms of reverence. With all his faults (but who is without them?), even Raphael bows before him."

In criticising a painting by Caracci, Allston used the following Dantesque sentences: "The subject was the body of the Virgin borne for interment by four apostles. The figures are colossal; the tone dark and of tremendous color. It seemed, as I looked at it, as if the ground shook at their tread, and the air were darkened by their grief."

Vanderlyn has told us how he and Allston, Turner and Fenimore Cooper, frequented the famous old Caffè Greco, the resort of the northern barbarians in Rome for so many decades. and the favorite haunt of Thorwaldsen and Cornelius, Andersen and Louis of Bavaria, Flaxman and Gibson, Shelley, Keats, and Byron. Thorwaldsen could hardly have been a student with Allston, as some assert, for he had been in Rome eight years when the latter arrived, and had already won rich pecuniary rewards and the praise of Canova. Nevertheless, he was a friend of the American artist, and often in after years pointed to him as a proof that the loftiest abilities were indigenous to the Western world.

Another group of eminent persons then living in Rome, and accessible to the young Carolinian, was gathered around William von Humboldt, the Prussian ambassador, and Alexander von Humboldt, who had just returned from his travels among the South-American Andes. The Danish envoy, Baron von Schubert, and the Neapolitan envoy, Cardinal Fesch, were also members of the artistic society of the city. Madame de Staël was living there at the same time, with A. W. von Schlegel and Sismondi.

During the period of Allston's sojourn at Rome, the city was continually menaced by the armies of Napoleon, which had occupied several of the Papal provinces. In February, 1808, the French troops entered the gates, disarming the Pontifical guards, and the States of the Church were converted into provinces of the Empire. Pope Pius VII. was imprisoned in the Quirinal Palace, but published thence a bull, excommunicating all who had commanded or were concerned in the invasion of the city. In July of the next year Pius was arrested by French officers and haled away to his prolonged captivity of five years at Savona and Fontainebleau.

The fascination which Allston exercised upon all around him was felt strongly by Washington Irving, who says: "I first became acquainted with Washington Allston early in the spring of 1805. He had just arrived from France, I from Sicily and Naples. I was then not quite twenty-two years of age, — he a little older. There was something to me inexpressibly fascinating in the appearance and manners of Allston. I do not think I have ever been more completely captivated on a first acquaintance. He was of a light and graceful form, with large blue eyes, and black silken hair, waving and curling round a pale, expressive countenance. Everything about him spoke the man of intellect and refinement. His conversation was copious, animated, and highly graphic; warmed by a genial sensibility and benevolence, and enlivened at times by a chaste and gentle humor. A young men's intimacy took place immediately between us, and we were much together during my brief sojourn at Rome. He was taking a general view of the place before settling himself down to his professional studies. We visited together some of the finest collections of paintings, and he taught me how to visit them to the most advantage, guiding me always to the masterpieces, and passing by the others without notice. 'Never attempt to enjoy every picture in a great collection,' he would say, 'unless you have a year to bestow upon it. You may as well try to enjoy every dish at a Lord Mayor's feast. Both mind and palate get confounded by a great variety and rapid succession, even of delicacies. The mind can only take in a certain number of images and impressions distinctly; by multiplying the number, you weaken each, and render the whole confused and vague. Study the choice pieces in each collection; look upon none else, and you will afterwards find them hanging up in your memory.'

"He was exquisitely sensitive to the graceful and the beautiful, and took great delight in paintings which excelled in color; yet he was strongly moved and roused by objects of grandeur. I well recollect the admiration with which he contemplated the sublime statue of Moses by Michael Angelo, and his mute awe and reverence on entering the stupendous pile of St. Peter's. Indeed, the sentiment of veneration, so characteristic of the elevated and poetic mind, was continually manifested by him. His eyes would dilate; his pale countenance would flush; he would breathe quick, and almost gasp in expressing his feelings, when excited by any object of grandeur and sublimity.

"We had delightful rambles together about Rome and its environs, one of which came near changing my whole course of life. We had been visiting a stately villa, with its gallery of paintings, its marble halls, its terraced gardens set out with statues and fountains, and were returning to Rome about sunset. The blandness of the air, the serenity of the sky, the transparent purity of the atmosphere, and that nameless charm which hangs about an Italian landscape, had derived additional effect from being shared with Allston, and pointed out by him with the enthusiasm of an artist. As I listened to him, and gazed upon the landscape, I drew in my mind a contrast between our different pursuits and prospects. He was to reside amid these delightful scenes, surrounded by masterpieces of art, by classic and historic monuments, by men of congenial minds and tastes, engaged like him in the constant study of the sublime and beautiful. I was to return home to the dry study of the law, for which I had no relish, and, as I feared, but little talent.

"Suddenly the thought presented itself, 'Why might I not remain here, and turn painter?' I had taken lessons in drawing before leaving America, and had been thought to have some aptness, as I certainly had a strong inclination for it. I mentioned the idea to Allston, and he caught at it with eagerness. Nothing could be more feasible. We would take an apartment together. He would give me all the instruction and assistance in his power, and was sure I would succeed.

"For two or three days the idea took full possession of my mind; but I believe it owed its main force to the lovely evening ramble in which I first conceived it, and to the romantic friendship I had formed with Allston. Whenever it recurred to mind, it was always connected with beautiful Italian scenery, palaces, and statues, and fountains, and terraced gardens, and Allston as the companion of my studio. I promised myself a world of enjoyment in his society, and in the society of several artists with whom he had made me acquainted, and pictured forth a scheme of life all tinted with the rainbow-hues of youthful promise.

"My lot in life, however, was differently cast. Doubts and fears gradually clouded over my prospect; the rainbow-tints faded away; I began to apprehend a sterile reality; so I gave up the transient but delightful prospect of remaining in Rome with Allston and turning painter."

The poet-painter says of another friend: "To no other man whom I have known do I owe so much *intellectually* as to Mr. Coleridge, with whom I became acquainted in Rome, and who has honored me with his friendship for more than five-and-twenty years. He used to call Rome the *silent* city; but I never could think of it as such, while with him; for, meet him when or where I would, the fountain of his mind was never dry, but, like the far-reaching aqueducts that once supplied this mistress of the world, its living stream seemed specially to flow for every classic ruin over which we wandered. And when I recall some of our walks under the pines of the Villa Borghese, I am almost tempted to dream that I had once listened to Plato in the groves of the Academy. It was there he taught me this golden rule: *never to judge of any work of art by its defects;* a rule as wise as benevolent; and one that while it has spared me much pain, has widened my sphere of pleasure."

Allston studied not only drawing and painting, but also modelling in clay, to which he devoted much time. He always kept up the practice of modelling, and recommended it to young painters as one of the best means of acquiring an accurate knowledge of the joints. In the study of anatomy he labored unremittingly, considering the relations of bones, joints, and muscles, and bestowing prolonged attention on the structure and peculiarities of the external human skin. He also gave himself eagerly to the study and analysis of the methods employed by the old masters in coloring.

His magical coloring attracted much attention, even in Rome. Twenty years later, when Weir was studying his profession in that city, the Italian artists asked after a countryman of his, for whom they had no other name than the *American Titian*. When Weir spoke the name of Allston, in calling the roll of American artists, they exclaimed, "That's the man!" This wonderful wealth of color was ever the grand distinction of the master, and was imbued with depth and richness and divine harmony. He made no secret of his processes and materials, but those who sought to avail themselves thereof found that they lacked the fine inner sense of color. His marvellous carnations were never even imitated. He was altogether dependent on his mastery of colors in simple landscapes and ideal female heads, where the charms of design and incident were absent, yet the sense of beauty is fully satisfied by the richness of the hues.

William Ware says: "When, after a careful study of very many of the best instances of Titian's pencil, I returned, and, with that experience fresh in my mind, again re-examined the best works of Allston, I felt that, in the great Venetian, I had found nothing more true, nothing more beautiful, nothing more perfect, than I had already seen in Allston." An able critic, in Bunsen's great work on Rome, avers that Allston's colors came nearer Titian's than those of any other modern artist. Sandby, the historian of the Royal Academy, says that "Allston was famous in Rome for rich color . . . obtained by an extensive use of asphaltum, after the manner of Rembrandt."

In 1805 the young art-student painted a portrait of himself, which he gave to his friend Mrs. N. Amory, of Newport. In this early work the connoisseur cannot fail to see intimations of the grace, vigor, and minute finish of the artist's later pictures, while the uncritical observer is charmed with the youthful sweetness of the face.

Two other small pictures which he painted at Rome were 'David playing the Harp before Saul' and 'The Romans and the Serpent of Epidaurus.'

In 1809 Allston returned to America, and remained in Boston for nearly two years, when he married the lady to whom he had long been engaged. She was Miss Ann Channing, the daughter of William Channing, a prominent lawyer of Newport, and granddaughter of William Ellery, a signer of the Declaration of Independence. She was thirty-one years old when Allston married her.

In a letter to Mr. Ellery, William Ellery Channing said: "A few hours ago Washington and Ann, after their long and patient courtship, were united in marriage. . . . Your granddaughter has found, I believe, an excellent husband, one who from principle and affection will make her happiness his constant object. I hope that she will settle at no great distance from us; but we have not yet sufficient taste for the arts to give Mr. Allston the encouragement he deserves."

During this sojourn at Boston the master wrote some of the poems which were afterwards published in "The Sylphs of the Seasons." They were read, in manuscript, by many of his personal friends, and called forth high praise. In 1811 he also read a poem before the Phi Beta Kappa of Harvard College. During this visit to America Allston received several visits from his old friend Irving, who was now getting fairly to work in literature.

About this time S. F. B. Morse, the son of Jedediah Morse, the celebrated geographer, graduated from Yale College, and went home to his father's parsonage at Charlestown, Mass. Ever since the fourth year of his age he had drawn and painted, unaided by instruction, and now he determined to adopt art as a profession. Allston, ever ready and even anxious to help young men in whom he saw the divine light of genius, sought him out and directed his first studies, awakening in his mind a loving reverence which time never changed.

It is said that Allston paid some attention to portrait-painting after his return to America, charging higher prices than Stuart, who received $150 for a kit-cat picture (28 by 36 inches) and $100 for a bust. He was once asked if he did n't find the need of rest, and answered, "No, I only require a change. After I paint a portrait I paint a landscape, and then a portrait again." His studio was in the premises on Court Street, between Brattle Street and Cornhill, where Smybert, Dean Berkeley's Scottish *protégé*, had painted eighty years before. Here Allston made portraits of several local celebrities.

Benjamin West once told Walter Channing that "Allston should never have left London. His course here was plain, — his success certain. Here was the proper ground for his labor. He should never have gone to America, — or if he went, it should only have been on a visit. Never should he have married. He was already married, — married to the Art. He should have married no other."

CHAPTER III.

Return to London. — Collins, Leslie, and Morse. — Sir George Beaumont. — West. — Coleridge and Southey. — Death of Mrs. Allston. — Paris. — Lord Egremont. — Irving. — Homeward Bound.

In the year 1811 the master once more turned his steps toward London, to refresh himself at the springs of the Royal Academy, and to feel again the stimulus of a healthy rivalry. Mrs. Allston was the companion of his journey and the joy of his new home. The good ship *Lydia* sailed from New York in July, 1811, bearing the Allstons and Morse, with eleven other passengers. After a voyage of twenty-six days the vessel reached Liverpool, and the Boston trio established themselves at the Liverpool-Arms Hotel. But they were hurried from the city by the Mayor's orders, since hostilities were then impending between Great Britain and the United States, and all Americans were regarded with suspicion. They set off for London in a post-chaise, and made the journey of two hundred miles in a week, although Mrs. Allston was in very poor health. The master immediately renewed his former friendship with West, to whom he introduced young Morse; and settled in lodgings at 49 London Street, visiting his young *protégé* every day, to talk and smoke a cigar with him. Soon afterwards Charles R. Leslie came across the ocean to begin those careful studies, by which he became one of the most famous historical painters of England.

Leslie speaks thus of the time when he and Morse were at London, in 1811: "Our Mentors were Allston and King; nor could we have been better provided: Allston, a most amiable and polished gentleman and a painter of the purest taste; and King, warm-hearted, sincere, sensible, prudent, and the strictest of economists." Leslie, then seventeen years old, was bitterly homesick for Philadelphia, and found it possible to be unhappy even in London, where in later years he attained such proud honors. Morse was a year or two older, and labored diligently in acquiring the art which his subsequent invention of the electric telegraph rendered him independent of.

The two youths lived together, in dreary rooms near Fitzroy Square, and visited Mrs. Siddons's performances and copied the Elgin Marbles in company. West and Allston were their instructors and advisers, permitting them to see all their pictures in various stages of progress, and helping them in many ways. Leslie says that "it was Allston who first awakened what little sensibility I may possess to the beauties of color. He first directed my attention to the Venetian school, particularly to the works of Paul Veronese, and taught me to see, through the accumulated dirt of ages, the exquisite charm that lay beneath. Yet for a long time I took the merit of the Venetians on trust, and, if left to myself, should have preferred works which I now feel to be comparatively worthless. I remember when the picture of 'The Ages,' by Titian, was first pointed out to me by Allston as an exquisite work, I thought he was laughing at me."

Allston was a severe teacher and an unflinching critic, as Morse shows in one of his letters home, saying: "Mr. Allston is our most intimate friend and companion. I can't feel too grateful to him for his attentions to me; he calls every day, and superintends all that we are doing. When I am at a stand and perplexed in some parts of the picture, he puts me right, and encourages me to proceed, by praising those parts which he thinks good; but he is faithful, and always tells me when anything is bad. It is mortifying, sometimes, when I have been painting all day very hard, and begin to be pleased with what I have done, and on showing it to Mr. Allston, with the expectation of praise, and not only of praise, but a score of 'excellents, well-dones, and admirables,' — I say, it is mortifying to hear him, after a long silence, say: 'Very bad, sir; that is not flesh, it is mud, sir; it is painted with brick-dust and clay.' I have felt, sometimes, ready to dash my palette-knife through it, and to feel at the moment quite angry with him; but a little reflection restores me. I see that Mr. Allston is not a *flatterer*, but a *friend*, and that, really to improve, I must see my *faults*. What he says after this always puts me in good humor again. He tells me to *put a few flesh-tints here, a few gray ones there, and to clear up such and such a part, by such and such colors;* and not only that, but takes the palette and brushes, and shows me how. In this way he assists me; I think it one of the greatest blessings that I am under his eyes. I don't know how many errors I might have fallen into if it had not been for his attentions."

Early in 1866 Professor Morse bought Leslie's portrait of Allston, and presented it to the National Academy of Design, saying: "There are associations in my mind with those two eminent and beloved names which appeal too strongly to me to be resisted. . . . Allston was more than any other person my master in art. Leslie was my life-long cherished friend and fellow-pupil, whom I loved as a brother. We all lived together for years in the closest intimacy and in the same house."

In the little coterie of which Allston was the head were found Charles B. King, the Rhode-Island artist; Leslie and Morse; Collard, the merry musician; and Lonsdale, a mediocre portrait-painter who made excellent company. Frequent were the evening parties at their houses, when they assembled for social pleasures and conversation. Leslie wrote to his sister that

"Mr. and Mrs. Allston are the only friends we have left that are very near us, and if I were to lose the society of Mr. Allston I should not wish to remain any longer in England." John Trumbull, the American historical painter, was then occupying a diplomatic post, and Allston said of him: "Among the many persons from whom I received attentions, during my residence in London, I must not omit Colonel Trumbull, who always treated me with the utmost courtesy."

In 1811 Leslie introduced Allston to William Collins, who was afterwards a Royal Academician, famous for his landscapes, marines, and *genre* pictures of rustic English children. The American artist became very intimate with the Collins family, and their friendship was kept up to the end of life. In the biography of William Collins, written by his illustrious son, Wilkie Collins, many of his most important mental acquisitions are referred to the effects of his intimacy with Allston and Coleridge. The great novelist thus characterizes the Carolinian artist: "To a profound and reflective intellect he united an almost feminine delicacy of taste and tenderness of heart, which gave a peculiar charm to his conversation, and an unusual eloquence to his opinions. . . . Mr. Collins owed to his short personal intercourse with this valued companion, not only much delightful communication on the Art, but the explanation of many religious difficulties under which his mind then labored, and the firm settlement of those religious principles which were afterwards so apparent in every action of his life."

About this time Sir George Beaumont, a friend of Sir Joshua Reynolds and an accomplished connoisseur, wrote a very complimentary letter to Allston, having seen the sketch of his great picture of 'The Dead Man Revived.' He requested the artist to paint another compostion for the new church at Ashby de la Zouch, for which he offered him £200. 'The Angel Delivering St. Peter from Prison' was the result of this commission, to which the artist devoted six months; and was much admired by the noble patron. At a later day, however, it was replaced by a stained window, and remanded to one of the garrets of Beaumont's mansion, whence it was rescued by Dr. Hooper, an American admirer of its author, and removed to Boston, and subsequently to the chapel of the Massachusetts Insane Asylum, at Worcester. The figures in this composition are larger than life, and the head of the angel is a portrait of Mrs. Allston. The highly finished study for the head of St. Peter was exhibited in Boston in 1837.

Allston said: "Among my English friends it is no disparagement to place at their head Sir George Beaumont. It is pleasant to think of my obligations to such a man, *a gentleman in his very nature.* Gentle, brilliant, generous, — I was going to attempt his character, but I will not; it was so peculiar and finely textured that I know but one man who could draw it, and that 's Coleridge, who knew him well, — to know whom was to honor."

Sir George was favored by the intimate friendship of Wordsworth, who first advised him to visit Allston, giving as a reason that Coleridge said that his picture of 'Cupid and Psyche' had not been surpassed in its coloring since the days of Titian. In 1815 Beaumont asked B. R. Haydon, Landseer's master, to go to Allston's studio and see the 'St. Peter.' Haydon commended Allston for having abandoned portraiture, and said that "next to knowing what one *can* do, the best acquisition for an artist is to know what he *can't*."

Early in 1813 Mr. and Mrs. Allston, with Leslie and Morse, enjoyed a pleasant trip to Hampton Court, where they doubtless studied the ancient pictures. At this time the brilliant young American actor and dramatist, John Howard Payne, was playing at the Drury-Lane Theatre with great success. He was a frequent and welcome guest of the Allstons, who had known him and his family very well in America. In the beautiful spring season Leslie, Morse, and the Allstons made a pleasant journey of ten days to Windsor, Oxford, and Blenheim Palace, enjoying uncommonly fine weather.

In 1813 Morse wrote the following appreciative sentences about his noble teacher: "I cannot close this letter without telling you how much I am indebted to that excellent man Mr. Allston; he is extremely partial to me, and has often told me that he is proud of calling me his pupil; he visits me every evening, and our conversation is generally upon the inexhaustible subject of our *divine* art, and upon *home*, which is next in our thoughts. I know not in what words to speak of Mr. Allston. I can truly say I do not know the slightest imperfection in him; he is amiable, affectionate, learned, possessed of the greatest powers of mind and genius, modest, unassuming, and, above all, a *religious* man. You may perhaps suppose that my partiality for him blinds me to his faults; but no man could conceal, on so long an acquaintance, every little foible from one constantly in his company; and, during the whole of my acquaintance with Mr. Allston, I never heard him speak a peevish word, or utter a single inconsiderate sentence; he is a man of whom I cannot speak sufficiently, and my love for him I can only compare to that love which ought to subsist between brothers. He is a man for whose genius I have the highest veneration, for whose principles I have the greatest respect, and for whose amiable properties I have an increasing love. . . . You must recollect, when you tell friends that I am studying in England, that I am a pupil of Mr. Allston, and not Mr. West; they will not long ask you who Mr. Allston is; he will very soon astonish the world. It is said by the greatest connoisseurs in England, who have seen some of Mr. Allston's works, that he is destined to revive the art of painting in all its splendor, and that no age ever boasted of so great a genius. It might be deemed invidious were I to make public another opinion of the first men in this country: it is, that Mr. Allston will almost as far surpass Mr. West as Mr. West has other artists, and this is saying a great deal, considering the very high standing which Mr. West enjoys at present."

During his abode in England Allston conformed to the custom of the country in regard to late dinners, finding it favorable also to his undisturbed studies. He dispensed with a midday meal, and worked incessantly, often amid great mental excitement, until his health was shattered by these unwonted fasts and toils. A serious and chronic derangement of the digestive organs ensued, from which he never wholly recovered; and his pure and enthusiastic spirit was henceforth chained to an inadequate physical constitution. His susceptible and highly nervous temperament was from this time hampered by material troubles, compelling him to long and frequent cessations from labor, and resulting in occasional inequalities of execution. But the rest given to the pencil was attended with an increased activity of the mind, while new themes for illumination were earnestly pondered, and new writings were prepared.

Allston's health became so seriously affected by his unremitting labors, that, after several months of great suffering, he was obliged to seek a revival by a change of air. He had an uncle living as the American Consul at Bristol, the city of Coleridge, Southey, Chatterton, Sydney Smith, and Robert Hall; and he hastened towards the adjacent watering-place of Clifton, in the hope that the medicinal waters might aid in his recovery. But when he reached Salt Hill, twenty-two miles from London, the malady grew so violent that he was unable to proceed farther, and was confined to a sick-bed for many days, tenderly cared for by his devoted wife. Morse and Leslie attended him in the journey, and the former hastened back to London, and brought Coleridge thence to Salt Hill. Leslie narrates how he occupied the same bed with the great poet, who spent the hours, when he dared to leave Allston's room, in a fascinated perusal of "Knickerbocker's History of New York." Once he left the sick-chamber at midnight, and took up "Knickerbocker's History of New York" ("only an American book"), and was found at ten o'clock the next forenoon still buried in its pages, with lights burning and shutters closed, unaware of the lapse of time. Coleridge discharged the utmost duties of friendship in a manner which was surprising in a person of such constitutional indolence, and thus manifested how ardent was his love for his artist-friend. As soon as Allston was able to be moved they carried him to Clifton, the picturesque and far-viewing western suburb of Brighton, whither Coleridge soon followed him. King, the eminent surgeon, Miss Edgeworth's brother-in-law, was then at Clifton; and Coleridge had induced Southey to write to him about the artist's case. His ministrations were so effectual that Allston ever afterwards attributed his escape from death to him (under Providence). But the process of recovery was slow and gradual, and the artist was subjected to great annoyance from his uncle, Vanderhorst, a kind-hearted and generous man, but gouty and crotchety, and filled with an inveterate animosity against doctors, "Don't let one of those rascals enter your door," he cried. "Follow my advice; live well, and trust to the air of Clifton. You see how well I am and how healthy all my family are, and this is because we never let a doctor come near us." Vanderhorst or some member of his family called frequently on their suffering kinsman, and Dr. King came twice daily, so that Leslie and Coleridge were forced to watch unceasingly lest the eccentric uncle should meet and assail the surgeon. King's visits were kept secret, and Vanderhorst took the whole credit of his nephew's recovery.

Probably no small part of the artist's improvement in health was due to the inspiration of the beautiful scenery of Clifton and the lower Avon River, beheld in the company of the cultured and sensitive Coleridge and Southey. While enjoying such society, amid these charming surroundings, Allston solaced the long weeks of his convalescence by composing several poems, which were published in London soon afterwards, in a duodecimo volume, entitled "The Sylphs of the Seasons." This volume was republished in Boston, in 1813, under the care of Professor Willard and Mr. Edmund T. Dana. An English author says that Allston also published in London a volume of "Hints to Young Practitioners in the Study of Landscape Painting." Nagler and Blanc both speak of this now forgotten book.

As soon as Allston had passed from under the stress of disease, though still an invalid, he returned to London, and finished the picture of 'The Dead Man Revived by Elisha's Bones.' This great work was exhibited at the British Institution in 1814, where it obtained the first prize of two hundred guineas; and was afterwards purchased by the Pennsylvania Academy of Fine Arts for $3,500. The master wrote to the friend who had managed the sale: "As necessary and acceptable as the money is to me, I assure you I think more of the honor conferred by the Academy becoming purchasers of my work." The composition is founded on 2 Judges xiii. 20—21: "And the bands of the Moabites invaded the land at the coming in of the year. And it came to pass as they were burying a man, that, behold, they spied a band of men, and they cast the man into the sepulchre of Elisha; and when the man was let down, and touched the bones of Elisha, he revived."

While the master was working on 'The Dead Man Revived' he devoted four months to the painting of a landscape, which he afterwards sent to Philadelphia, to be sold for two hundred guineas. He also painted a 'Mother and Child,' which was at first intended to represent the Madonna, but, failing to reach the artist's ideal, received a less pretentious title. He thought this one of his best pictures, and presented it to his friend McMurtrie, of Philadelphia. This gentleman also had some correspondence with Allston about a picture of 'Christ Healing in the Temple,' which the artist had designed and partly executed, but desisted from when convinced of the inadequacy of the composition. He wrote: "I may here observe that the universal failure of all painters, ancient and modern, in their attempts to give even a tolerable idea of the Saviour, has now determined me never to attempt it. Besides, I think His character too holy and sacred to be attempted by the pencil." Again, he said, when asked why he had not painted Christ: "I have not done so, because of my convictions concerning the nature, the mission, and the character of the Saviour. These exalt Him so far beyond such an apprehension as could alone enable me to communicate any idea of Him I may strive to reach, that I should fail if I attempted it. I could not make Him a study for art."

During this year, 1814, Leslie introduced Allston to John Martin, "the painter of architectural dreams," whose works were filled with poetic fascination, terrible and brilliant weirdness, and startling imagination. The American had strongly desired to know Martin, ever since he had seen his picture of 'Sadak Seeking the Waters of Oblivion.' Says Martin: "Thus, twenty years ago, commenced a friendship which caused me deeply to regret Allston's departure for his native country; for I have rarely met a man whose cultivated and refined taste, combined with a mild yet enthusiastic temper and honorable mind, more excited my admiration and esteem."

When the master was painting 'The Dead Man Revived,' he was visited by West, who exclaimed, "Why, sir, this reminds me of the fifteenth century; you have been studying in the highest school of art. There are eyes in this country that will be able to see so much excellence." He also noticed a head which Allston had modelled in clay for one of his figures, and, taking it for an antique, asked whose it was. Upon finding by whom it had been modelled, he carefully examined it, and expressed his opinion that no sculptor in England could do as well. Leslie says: "I never was more delighted in my life than when I heard this praise coming from Mr. West, and so perfectly agreeing with my own opinion of Allston. He has been in high spirits ever since, and his picture has advanced amazingly rapid for these two or three days."

West was delighted with Allston's 'Diana,' which was exhibited at the British Gallery in 1814, and said to his son, "There, there, why, there is nobody who does anything like that." Young West answered, "It looks like a bit of Titian." "O, yes," exclaimed the venerable artist, "that's Titian's flesh, that's Titian's flesh." He commended the landscape, composition, drawing, and coloring; and advised his gifted compatriot to follow it with others of similar small size and delicate finish. About this same time Allston painted the head of West, for the portrait which is now in the Boston Museum of Fine Arts. Inness says: "How real seems that portrait alongside of Stuart's pink fancy of Washington! and what a piece of bosh, by contrast, is the 'Portrait of Benjamin West, Esq.' (I believe he was n't 'Sir'd'), 'President of the Royal Academy,' by Sir Thomas Lawrence."

In the autumn of 1814 Allston dwelt at Bristol, and was busily engaged in portrait-painting, meeting with indifferent success. Leslie wrote deploring the absence of the master's family and Morse from London, and saying that it made him feel "as I used to when away from my mother and sisters." Allston's uncle was the only purchaser of his pictures, so that Morse said that he might have starved for all the Bristol people did to help him. But among the few portraits which he had executed he ranked those of Coleridge and Dr. King, painted at this time, as the best. Wordsworth said of the former, "It is the only likeness that ever gave me any pleasure." It was painted for Mr. Josiah Wade, and is now in the British National Portrait Gallery. Allston himself wrote: "So far as I can judge of my own production, the likeness is a true one, but it is Coleridge in repose; and, though not unstirred by the perpetual ground-swell of his ever-working intellect, and shadowing forth something of the deep philosopher, it is not Coleridge in his highest mood, the poetic state. When in that state, no face I ever saw was like to his; it seemed almost spirit made visible, without a shadow of the visible upon it. Could I then have fixed it upon canvas! But it was beyond the reach of my art."

It is said that at this same period Allston painted a portrait of Robert Southey, another of the great lake poets. He also executed two or three fancy compositions, but no trace of them can now be found. Another portrait of this period represented Mrs. King, the surgeon's wife, who was of the Edgeworth family, so famous in the literature of that day.

Southey developed a warm intimacy with Allston, and frequently conversed with him about artistic and literary subjects. "Have you many old books in your country?" said he, one day. "If not, I could not live there." He told Collins

that some of Allston's poems were among "the finest productions of modern times." Coleridge once said to Thomas Campbell that our master had "poetic and artistic genius unsurpassed by any man of his age." He also called him "the first genius produced by the Western world."

Allston's poem, "America to Great Britain," which Charles Sumner calls "one of the choicest lyrics in the language," received the honor of being incorporated by Coleridge in his volume of "Sibylline Leaves," which was published in 1817. Our own Longfellow now possesses the author's copy of this book, enriched by numerous marginal notes in the handwriting of the great lake poet, among which we find, alongside of the "America to Great Britain," the following sentence, in Coleridge's delicate chirography: "By Washington Allston, a painter born to renew the fifteenth century." Coleridge was very fond of hearing the artist's weird and wonderful stories of the supernatural, and in after years frequently repeated one of them, whose scene was laid at Harvard College. In the text of the "Sibylline Leaves" Coleridge printed, as a note to the "America to Great Britain": "This poem, written by an American gentleman, a valued and dear friend, I communicate to the reader for its moral no less than its patriotic spirit."

Allston now returned to London, and took a house on Tinney Street, which he furnished and fitted for his home. But it was ordained that his cherished dreams of domestic joys in the new domicile should fail of realization, and in their place should arise one of the profoundest sorrows of his life. Mrs. Allston had been incessant in her care over her husband's sickness, and returned to London with impaired health. After entering the new house her illness became very serious, and she died within two or three days. Leslie says: "She was never tired of talking of 'that little saint, William,' as she called him. The very clay of which the Channings were formed seemed to have religion in its composition. Mrs. Allston told me that her brother, when a child, used to turn a chair into a pulpit, and preach little sermons to the other children of the family. I saw Channing often during his short stay in London, — and to see him was to love him. At his request I accompanied him to the burying-ground of St. Pancras Chapel, to show him his sister's grave." The only persons present at her funeral were her husband, Leslie, Morse, and John Howard Payne. The bereaved painter wrote to a friend, "The death of my wife left me nothing but my art, which then seemed to me as nothing."

Morse wrote home, saying: "Mrs. Allston, the wife of our beloved friend, died last evening, and the event overwhelmed us all in the deepest sorrow. As for Mr. Allston, for several hours after the death of his wife he was almost bereft of his reason. Mr. Leslie and I are applying our whole attention to him, and we have so far succeeded as to see him more composed."

When Mrs. Allston had passed away, the pleasant prospects of the future life in the new house seemed to have died with her, and the grieving artist soon abandoned a place whose memories were so painful. He went into lodgings in Buckingham Place, Fitzroy Square, where Leslie and Morse were living, in the centre of the artists' quarter of London. Suffering under extreme depression of spirits, his long and sleepless nights were haunted by horrid thoughts, and diabolical imprecations forced themselves into his mind.

Sincerely religious as he was, he was profoundly distressed by these visitations, and desired Leslie to consult Coleridge about his case. The great poet was found walking bareheaded in the garden at Highgate, and told Leslie: "Allston should say to himself, '*Nothing is me but my will.* These thoughts, therefore, that force themselves on my mind, are no part of *me*, and there can be no guilt in them.' If he will make a strong effort to become indifferent to their recurrence, they will either cease, or cease to trouble him." Much more he said, in sympathy with the sensitive and suffering artist; and his messages were blessed in the peace which their suggestions procured for the unfortunate Allston. He also sought for consolation from a higher source, and was confirmed as a member of the Episcopal Church.

In 1815 Morse wrote of his master: "I never felt so low-spirited as when he was ill. I often thought, if he should be taken away at this time what an irreparable loss it would be, not only to me, but to America and to the world. Oh! he is an angel on earth. I cannot love him too much. Excuse my warmth; I never can speak of Mr. Allston but in raptures."

Washington Irving visited him frequently, and wrote: "Allston was dejected in spirits from the loss of his wife, but I thought a dash of melancholy had increased the amiable and winning graces of his character. I used to pass long evenings with him and Leslie; indeed Allston, if any one would keep him company, would sit up until cock-crowing, and it was hard to break away from the charms of his conversation. He was an admirable story-teller; for a ghost-story, none could surpass him. He acted the story as well as told it."

During the summer of 1816 Allston painted a picture of 'Rebecca at the Well,' which the London artists called one of his best works. He sent it to his friend, Mr. Van Schaick, of New York. The exhibition of this year contained his 'Morning in Italy'; and the preceding one had been adorned with the 'Donna Mencia in the Robbers' Cave' (*Gil Blas*, Book I. Chap. X.).

The scrupulous and sensitive conscience of the master is illustrated by an incident occurring at this time. He was in urgent need of money, and had recently found a purchaser for one of his pictures. But when he thought the matter over, alone, at evening, he concluded that the subject of the painting was such that it might some time have an immoral effect on some perverted imagination. He immediately went to his patron's house and paid back the money, after which he took the picture home and destroyed it.

In September, 1817, Allston went to Paris, *via* Brighton and Dieppe, in company with Leslie and William Collins. They all made studies in the Louvre, and visited the houses of the chief artists of the city. Gérard was the only one who received them in person, and even he did not show them his pictures. Leslie has described the keen appreciation with which the party visited Notre Dame and the Louvre. Allston stayed in the French capital six weeks, and then returned to London.

Of the trip to Paris Collins wrote: "During this visit I had of course the very best opportunities of becoming acquainted with my friend's real character, which, in every new view I took of it, became more satisfactory. The sweetness and subdued cheerfulness of his temper, under the various little inconveniences of our journey, was much to be admired; and his great reverence for sacred things, and the entire purity and innocence of his conversation (coupled, as it was, with power of intellect and imagination), I never saw surpassed. Blessed be God, these qualities, these gifts, were effectual to the pulling down of many strongholds and vain imaginations on my part. How then can I be too grateful to Heaven for my acquaintance with one to whom, and to whose example, I owe so much? It is a source of great comfort to me to know, that although we were for so many years separated by the Atlantic, he yet sometimes spoke of me; and especially that so short a time before his death he had me in mind."

In December he sent his regards to Irving, in Leslie's letter, wherein allusions are made to the illustrations to "The Sketch Book" and "Knickerbocker's History," which Allston and Leslie had contracted to design. The former furnished but one of the eleven illustrations, a representation of Wouter Van Twiller deciding a lawsuit. At this time Allston had just finished 'The Angel Uriel in the Sun,' from which he omitted the positive colors of red, blue, and yellow, and yet produced a picture of rich and glowing tone. The angel's figure is colossal, though foreshortened to a height of but nine feet; and his air and attitude are very noble and heroic. The British Institution gave the artist a prize of one hundred and fifty guineas, on account of the picture, which Leslie held as equal to the best works of Paul Veronese.

It is said that one day he heard a knock at the studio door, and arose to admit the visitor, who desired to know where his picture of 'Uriel' could be found. Allston brought out the glowing canvas from a dusty corner of the studio, and, when urged to state his price, declined, saying that he had often done so, and found none willing to pay it. "Would £400 be an adequate sum?" asked the visitor; and when the amazed artist said that that was more than he had ever asked, he gladly took the picture at that price. This generous patron was the Marquis of Stafford, who was ever afterward a warm friend and protector of Allston.

Under the inspiration of his artistic surroundings in London, Allston worked with marvellous rapidity. The 'Uriel' was finished in six weeks, and he said, "I painted it at a heat,— for the Royal Academy Exhibition." The 'Elijah' was done in only three weeks. The 'Belshazzar,' the source of most of the master's failure, was sketched out before April, 1817. During the same year he painted the 'Clytie,' and at the Exhibition of 1818 he was represented by a Shakespearian scene, 'Hermia and Helena.' Another work of this period was the 'Falstaff and his Ragged Recruits,' a picture about four feet long and containing a dozen figures, most of which were portraits of actors then on the English stage.

Flaxman once said to Allston, upon being complimented on his designs from Homer and Dante, "I will now show you the sources of many of them"; and proceeded to lay before him a great variety of sketches from nature, which he had made in the streets and houses of London. Flaxman lived in the next house to that of Allston, on Fitzroy Square, and was very intimate with his genial neighbor.

While Abernethy was at the summit of his popularity Allston called on him to be treated for a pain in his thigh, and was met at the door by a coarse-looking and shaggy-headed person, whom he took for a servant. "Come in, come in, mon," said this uncouth fellow, with a harsh Scotch accent; to whom the amazed artist answered, "But Mr. Abernethy may be engaged; perhaps I had better call another time." "Come in, mon, I say," rejoined the person at the door; and pulling the visitor in, planted himself against the closed door, and added, "Now tell me what is your business with Mr. Abernethy,— I am Mr. Abernethy." Allston said, "I have come to consult you about an affection—" "What the de'il hae I to do with your affections?" cried the blunt Scot; and the gentle patient timidly rejoined, "Perhaps, Mr. Abernethy, you are engaged at present, and I had better call again." "De'il the bit, mon, de'il the bit,— come in, come in," said the great surgeon; and led Allston and the attendant Morse into his office, where he examined and prescribed for the case with marvellous tenderness and skill.

After returning from Paris, Allston completed his picture of 'Jacob's Dream,' wherein a vast multitude of angels is seen, and the ladder to heaven appears as "immeasurable flights of steps, with platform above platform, rising and extending into space immeasurable." Lord Egremont purchased this picture, and told Leslie that the figures therein reminded him more of Raphael than anything else he had seen by any modern artist. He was as much pleased with the artist as with his pictures, and gave him an urgent invitation to partake of the noble hospitalities of Petworth Castle, whose gates were ever open wide to men of genius. He visited the castle, and perhaps met Turner and Chantrey or some other of the artists who were such frequent guests there. He became an ardent admirer of Turner, whom he characterized as the greatest painter since the days of Claude.

In 1836 Freeman and Leslie visited Petworth, and found the 'Jacob's Dream' in the garrets of the mansion; while in the Earl's library were two of Allston's daintiest cabinet-pictures. Leslie did not class the 'Jacob's Dream' with the best works of its author, though Tom Taylor says that it was his masterpiece. The Earl said of 'The Repose in Egypt,' that it was "transcendent in every artistic quality."

In March, 1819, Coleridge wrote to Leslie, inviting him to visit his house, and closing thus: "Are we not always *delighted* to see you? Now, too, more than ever, since, in addition to yourself, you are all we have of Allston." During the latter part of his sojourn in England, the artist had frequently visited the poet in the secluded asylum at Highgate, near London, where he was endeavoring, under Dr. Gilman's care, to free himself from the opium-habit. Here he used to meet Charles Lamb and other friends, and join in their intellectual conversations.

When Coleridge's tragedy of "Remorse" was first played, its author occupied a box near the stage, with Allston, Morse, Leslie, King, and Charles Lamb as his guests. In April, 1818, the master dined with Lamb, Haydon, and H. C. Robinson, and the latter said of him: "Allston has a mild manner, a soft voice, and a sentimental air with him, — not at all Yankeeish; but his conversation does not indicate the talent displayed in his paintings."

The Earl of Egremont had introduced himself to Allston, and became one of his most munificent patrons. Before he left England he said to him, "I hear you are going to America, — I am sorry for it. Well, if you do not meet with the encouragement which you deserve, in your own country, we shall all be very glad to see you back again."

It has been said that when Allston was in London he always ceased to work after he had made a popular sensation with some great picture, and the public heard no more of him for long periods, during which he rested himself by social recreation. Instead of following up the effect of a success, and keeping his name before the people, he gave himself up to long evenings of story-telling, at which he was unrivalled, and richly entertained his many friends with his delightful anecdotes and original tales. He was not accustomed to retire early, and his rest was eked out by sleeping until late in the morning. These intervals of *dolce far niente* were not the outgrowth of sluggishness or coldness towards his art, but were necessitated by his physical limitations and the lassitude following extraordinary efforts. Towards evening his spirits usually brightened, and until midnight flowed free and sparkling.

Men of taste and admirers of Allston's style have lamented his return to America, believing that if he had remained abroad, enjoying the stimulus of the sympathy and fellowship of the great British artists and literati, he might have advanced to a lofty position among the European disciples of art, and awakened still further the genial interest and patronage of the insular nobility. But Irving was one of those who advised him to return home, arguing that it was better to be the foremost artist in America than one among the many masters in Europe.

Late in July, 1818, Irving wrote to Leslie: "I shall try hard to see Allston before he sails.... I regret exceedingly that he goes to America, now that his prospects are opening so promisingly in this country; but perhaps it is all for the best. His 'Jacob's Dream' was a particular favorite of mine. I have gazed on it again and again, and the more I gazed the more I was delighted with it. I believe if I was a painter, I could at this moment take a pencil and delineate the whole, with the attitude and expression of every figure."

Irving once wrote: "The road to fame and fortune was now open to Allston; he had but to remain in England, and follow up the signal impression he had made. Unfortunately, previous to this recent success, he had been disheartened by domestic affliction, and by the uncertainty of his pecuniary prospects, and had made arrangements to return to America. I arrived in London a few days before his departure, full of literary schemes, and delighted with the idea of our pursuing our several arts in fellowship. It was a sad blow to me to have this day-dream again dispelled. I urged him to remain and complete his grand painting of 'Belshazzar's Feast,' the study of which gave promise of the highest kind of excellence. Some of the best patrons of the art were equally urgent. He was not to be persuaded, and I saw him depart with still deeper and more painful regret than I had parted with him in our youthful days at Rome. I think our separation was a loss to both of us, — to me a grievous one. The companionship of such a man is invaluable. For his own part, had he remained in England for a few years longer, surrounded by everything to encourage and stimulate him, I have no doubt he would have been at the head of his art. He appeared to me to possess more than any contemporary the spirit of the old masters; and his merits were becoming widely appreciated."

Irving had such a high opinion of his friend's critical ability that he read to him the manuscript of "The Sketch-Book," to draw forth his comments thereon. The author felt a doubt as to whether he had better publish the Legend of Sleepy Hollow, but Allston conferred a lasting favor on American literature by persuading him to do so.

Says Allston: "Next to my own country, I love England, the land of my ancestors. I should indeed be ungrateful if I did not love a country from which I have never received other than kindness; in which, even during the late war, I was never made to feel that I was a foreigner. By the English artists, among whom I number some of my most valued friends, I was uniformly treated with openness and liberality. Out of the art, too, I found many fast and generous friends.

"Leslie, Irving, and Sir Thomas Lawrence were the last persons I shook hands with on leaving London. Irving and Leslie had accompanied me to the stage, and Sir Thomas, who was passing by on his morning ride, kindly stopped to offer me his good wishes. It is pleasant to have the last interview with those whom we wish to remember associated with kind feelings."

The homeward-bound artist crossed the ocean in the ship *Galen*, and met with much tempestuous weather. During the height of one of the worst gales of the season he remained on deck, engaged in argument with the captain as to whether two-thirds of the ship's keel was not thrown clear of the sea at one time, and maintaining an unperturbed demeanor amid the terrors of the storm. He sketched the *Galen* as he supposed that she appeared in the heaviest seas.

CHAPTER IV.

The Studio at Boston. — Chester Harding. — Academic Honors. — Horatio Greenough. — Washington Irving. — De Veaux. — Morse.

HEAR Allston's own sentences: "A homesickness, which (in spite of some of the best and kindest friends, and every encouragement that I could wish as an artist) I could not overcome, brought me back to my own country in 1818. We made Boston Harbor on a clear evening in October. It was an evening to remember! The wind fell and left our ship almost stationary on a long low swell, as smooth as glass, and undulating under one of our gorgeous autumnal skies like a prairie of amber. The moon looked down upon us like a living thing, as if to bid us welcome, and the fanciful thought is still in my memory that she broke her image on the water to make partners for a dance of fire-flies, — and they *did* dance, if I ever saw dancing. Another thought recurs: that I had returned to a mighty empire, —

that I was in the very waters which the gallant *Constitution* had first broken, whose building I saw while at college, and whose 'slaughter-breathing brass,' to use a quotation from worthy Cotton Mather's Magnalia, *but now* ' grew hot and spoke' *her name* among the nations."

At that time Boston was a compact little city, of about 40,000 inhabitants, with a lucrative trade to the East Indies and other remote shores, and enjoying a dignified leisure which was undisturbed by the intense commercial activities of to-day. There were no such wide chasms between the different divisions of society as now exist, for there were no princely families on the one side, nor paupers on the other. Many of the aristocrats had expatriated themselves when the royal armies abandoned the city; and most of those who remained were slowly and peacefully laying the foundations of future social dynasties.

Allston's studio was established in the large barn on John Prince's estate, near the northwest corner of High Street and Pearl Street, and in close proximity to the houses of the Quincys, Perkinses, and Parsonses. His rooms were on Sister Street, which ran out of Federal Street near Dr. Channing's church, and he got his meals at the celebrated restaurant of Rouillard, the successor of Monsieur Julien, at the corner of Milk and Congress Streets.

On Chester Harding's return from Europe he settled in Boston, and says, in his "Egotistography": "I had now become intimately acquainted with Mr. Allston. His habits were peculiar in many respects. He lived alone, dining at six o'clock, and sitting up far into the night. He breakfasted at eleven or twelve. He usually spent three or four evenings, or rather nights, at my house every week; and I greatly enjoyed his conversation, which was of the most polished and refined order, and always instructive. I sometimes called at his studio. It was an old barn, very large, and as cheerless as any anchorite could desire. He never had it swept, and the accumulation of the dust of many years was an inch deep. You could see a track, leading through it to some remote corner of the room, as plainly as in new-fallen snow. He saw few friends in his room; lived almost in solitude, with only his own great thoughts to sustain him."

Early in 1819 Allston wrote to Morse, saying:

"Something like encouragement seems to appear in our horizon; and if we have any talents, we owe something to our country when she is disposed to foster them." At the same time he received an official communication from the secretary of the Royal Academy, stating that he had been elected an associate of that body, attended with congratulatory letters from Leslie and Collins. He was justly proud of having obtained this signal honor without canvassing, or begging for votes. A few years later, on the occurrence of a vacancy, he would have been appointed an Academician, but that the laws of the Royal Academy forbade that honor to persons who were not residents of the United Kingdom.

In November he received another letter from Collins, congratulating him on his election to the Academy, and sending him kind messages from Wordsworth, Southey, Coleridge, and Sir George Beaumont. In his answer, Allston excuses a delay, on the plea of his well-known habits of procrastination, and says: "I assure you I have written you at least twenty letters *in my head*, whilst I have been smoking my usual evening cigar." He thus expresses his gratification at the election to the Academy: "To my countrymen here, who value highly all foreign honors, it seems to have given almost as much pleasure as if it had been bestowed on the country; it must, therefore, be no small aid to my professional interests." He adds that there is no probability of his returning to England, since he had already met with most liberal patronage in Boston, and hoped to found there an English school of art. He believed there was a quicker appreciation of art among the Americans than in any other country.

About this time Allston was one of the leaders in the movement which resulted in a statue of Washington, by Chantrey, being placed in the Massachusetts State House; and was frequently in communication with the jovial old sculptor, who had been his friend while in England.

Allston's position on the vexed question of his day was clearly defined on his return from Europe, when he found that his step-father had recently died, having bequeathed him a young negro woman named Diana. Instead of selling her in the Charleston slave-market, for such a sum as would have delighted an impecunious artist, he immediately emancipated her, and gave her the legal free papers.

Allston had a violent dislike to President Jackson, and once declined to paint a battle in which he commanded, in terms almost of anger. Governor Hamilton of South Carolina induced Governor Everett of Massachusetts to attempt his good offices in softening the obdurate painter, but in vain.

The Allstons of South Carolina frequently visited New England, and during one of these sojourns the Hon. John A. Allston persuaded Morse, his kinsman's *protégé*, to go to Charleston and open a studio. There the young artist met with great success, both socially and professionally, and remained five months, painting sixty-two portraits. John A. Allston owned a fine picture-gallery, and had Morse portray his lovely daughter for it, draped in white, ordering the addition of "the most superb landscape you are capable of designing." The artist afterwards presented his patron with the great painting of 'The Judgment of Jupiter.' After Morse's marriage he returned to Charleston, where he acted as the agent of his old master in disposing of certain pictures, and kept up an interesting correspondence with him.

Governor R. F. W. Allston several times asked his famous kinsman to paint him a picture, but the only answer would be, " Robert, I must paint for money,"— as if the idea of taking money from a relative was quite out of the reach of possibility.

In July, 1821, Allston became acquainted with Thomas Sully, the eminent portrait-painter, who spent several months in Boston, making a highly finished copy of Mr. Wiggin's picture of 'The Capuchin Chapel,' painted by Granet. The master was also a friend of Gilbert Stuart, then nearly seventy years old, and in 1828 wrote an eloquent and appreciative eulogy upon him, for the *Daily Advertiser*.

When Dr. Channing went to Europe, in 1822, he carried a letter of introduction from Allston to Coleridge, and made such an impression upon the latter that he spoke of the great Boston divine as "a philosopher in both the possible renderings of the word, having the love of wisdom and the wisdom of love." This celebrated phrase he used in a letter to Allston, telling of his walks and talks with Channing.

Horatio Greenough entered Harvard University in 1821, and was soon made acquainted with Allston, who became his master and intimate companion. The cravings of the enthusiastic youth for a life of noble achievement in art, sometime coldly treated by practical friends, were revived and stimulated in the presence of the lofty soul and earnest purpose of the great painter, and a marvellous sympathy grew up between the two. Greenough dwelt with Edmund Dana, and met Allston there every Saturday, when he was accustomed to visit his kinsman. Dana was endowed with fine critical taste and a profound knowledge of art and literature; and the young student gladly hailed the approach of every seventh day, when he could listen to the inspiring conversation of such serene and benevolent sages. Greenough's mind was as elevated and as finely tempered as his form was heroic and symmetrical; and Allston, rejoicing to find so genial and respectful an auditor, impressed on his susceptible spirit a lofty ideal of art, a feeling of the dignity of his chosen profession, courage to meet its disciplining trials, and faith in the ultimate reward. These frequent meetings between the spiritual and prophet-like artist and the radiant young disciple were heavy with destiny for the latter, who wrote, many years later: "Allston was to me a father in what concerned my progress of every kind. He taught me first how to discriminate, how to think, how to feel. Before I knew him, I felt strongly, but blindly; and if I should never pass mediocrity, I should attribute it to my absence from him, so adapted did he seem to kindle and enlighten me, making me no longer myself, but, as it were, an emanation from his own soul." During his last visit to America the great sculptor said, with emotion, that the only thought which cast a shadow over his heart was that Allston was dead.

Percival's poem on "The Mind," delivered before the Connecticut Phi Beta Kappa in 1825, closed with a lament that America should permit so great an artist as Allston to be forced to earn his living in painting small sentimental pictures, while his greater capabilities were undeveloped.

In 1827 Allston received a favorable introduction to a wider circle of admirers, on displaying several of his pictures in the exhibition at the Boston Athenæum. Among these were the Jeremiah, Miriam, Florimel, and Valentine. He was now entering on what many admirers call his philosophical system of painting, to which he devoted the last sixteen years of his life.

In 1828 William Collins induced Allston to act as godfather by proxy to his second son, who was named William Allston Collins; and many years later Collins wrote to Dana: "I desire no better thing for him than that he may follow the example of his namesake, both as a painter and as a man." Mr. W. A. Collins is now celebrated as an accomplished author.

In 1829 Allston was asked to take as a pupil young De Veaux, of South Carolina, but declined, with the statement that he was not accustomed to receive students. He advised that his young compatriot should be placed with Chester Harding; but Inman and Sully had the honor of teaching "the gifted, the generous, the lost De Veaux." Two years before his short life closed, the art-student wrote, from Italy: "SULLY is our REYNOLDS, and ALLSTON our WONDER,—I would not give him for less than Michael Angelo! He is as fine as all the old masters together."

Washington Irving visited Allston in 1830, and found him "in the gray evening of life, apparently much retired from the world." He characterized him as "a man whose memory I hold in reverence and affection, as one of the purest, noblest, and most intellectual beings that ever honored me with his friendship." Mr. Dix, the last visitor at Sunnyside, a week before Irving's death, in 1859, chanced to speak of Allston, and thus describes the effect of that sweetly remembered name: "It set his soul all glowing with tender, affectionate enthusiasm. To hear the great painter so praised by the great writer, with a voice tremulous partly with infirmity but more with emotion, was something to keep as surely as if every word had been engraven with the point of a diamond."

George W. Flagg was one of Allston's best-beloved pupils, and one of whom he prophesied: "That boy, if I mistake not, will do great things one of these days. A great thing in his favor is, that his heart is as good as his head." The youth was also a relative of his master, since Allston's mother was his own grandmother. He was born at New Haven, but passed his boyhood at Charleston, S. C., where he developed his artistic tastes at a very early age, and made a remarkable portrait of Bishop England when he was but fourteen years old. He remained nearly two years under the care of the great master, enjoying his affectionate instructions and lofty conversation, and learning not only the technic of his art but also of its noble treasures and vast possibilities. The teacher and pupil were frequently seen walking together, the former impressing high truths on his disciple's mind by doctrine, analogy, and incident. The religious tendencies and conscientious aims of art were developed in every way, with the necessity for aspiration and industry; and the youth was instructed in the characters of the interesting men and beautiful women of Europe. One of Allston's sweetest poems was written for his kinsman, designing to show him that the elevated mind could find no satisfaction in mere pleasure, sought for itself alone. He also restrained him from inconsiderate criticism and the thoughtless dogmatism of an unripened mind.

Flagg designed 'A Boy listening to a Ghost-Story' and 'A Young Greek' while under Allston's care; and at length painted 'Jacob and Rachel at the Well,' whose merit was acknowledged by the master in the words, "Now you may consider yourself an artist." Afterwards Flagg executed noteworthy pictures in Boston, New Haven, and London; but was prevented by ill health from gaining the eminence which he might otherwise have attained.

Flagg was with Allston when he was painting the 'Spalatro,' and testifies to the rapt attention with which the artist regarded his work. He frequently showed his nervous sympathy for the characters he was portraying, by starting back from the canvas and assuming the attitude of the figure he was designing. This manner of instinctive imitation was a constant habit of the artist's, and illustrated his keen perception of the sentiment under treatment, and his thorough engrossment, physical and mental, in his work.

Another of Allston's pupils was Jared B. Flagg, George's brother, whose artistic career lasted nearly twenty years, or until 1854, when he took orders in the Episcopal Church. He was a member of the National Academy, and executed several highly praised ideal works, besides many portraits. Nor have his later pastoral duties prevented him from making numerous excellent pictures, and taking an active interest in the Yale College Art Gallery.

Richard M. Staigg was another young artist who was enriched by Allston's counsel and encouragement, which he won by his beautiful miniature of Mrs. Amory, of Newport. Staigg was brought up at Newport, where he was acquainted with the relatives of Stuart and Malbone; and studied the rich scale of colors on the palette of the former, and the exquisite miniature, 'The Hours,' of the latter. Allston's instruction was highly beneficial to his young disciple, who became eminent not only as a portrait-painter but also as a designer of vigorous and refined ideal pictures. One of his most delicate and memorable miniatures portrays the grand face of Allston; and two others, representing Webster and Everett, have been exquisitely engraved.

The 'Elijah in the Desert' is a large picture, perhaps 6 × 4 feet in size, which Allston painted in London and brought home with him. In this great work the chief feature is a sublime and illimitable desert-landscape, covered with rocks and sand, bounded by black mountains, and overhung with lowering clouds. The scene is dark and melancholy, but impressive in its calmness and silence. Elijah is a minor figure in the picture, and is hidden away among the grotesque and distorted roots of an enormous banyan-tree, the only tree in the whole wide landscape, and that dead and leafless. Hereunder flows the brook Cherith; and the ravens fly down with food for the outcast prophet. It has been said that this picture would have been far greater if Elijah and his whimsical tree had been omitted, leaving only the vast and solitary expanse of the desert.

This composition was painted with colors ground in milk, then varnished with copal, and retouched in oil-colors. It remained at the house of Allston's friend, Isaac P. Davis, until it was purchased (for $ 1,500) by an English tourist, the Hon. Mr. Labouchere, M. P., who carried it home. In 1870 Mrs. S. Hooper, of Boston, repurchased the 'Elijah' (for $ 4,000), and gave it to the Boston Museum of Fine Arts.

The 'Jeremiah' is a large and splendidly colored picture, 8 × 5 feet in size, and is founded on the thirty-sixth chapter of the Prophecy of Jeremiah. There are but two figures, those of the Prophet and Baruch his scribe. The former is sitting with his head majestically upraised, and lifts his right arm toward heaven, with the two middle fingers of the hand bent down and the others pointing upward, as if arrested suddenly and unconsciously. The head is the noblest and the expression the loftiest that Allston ever executed, nor could we imagine a more worthy conception as issuing from even Angelo's brain. The unsandalled right foot of the Prophet is one of the most noteworthy parts of the picture; and the temple architecture in the background, and the partly draped stone jar in the foreground, are executed with rare skill, the former in its aerial perspective and the latter in its Flemish minuteness of finish. Baruch's graceful figure is back to the spectator, sitting in the shadow, and bending over his tablets as if enthusiastically recording the Prophet's words.

The 'Jeremiah' has been likened to Beethoven's Fifth Symphony, or to a rich sunset, in the harmony with which its manifold tints are blended into a delicious unity. Some critics esteem it as the greatest painting by Allston's hand. It was retained for fifty years by Miss Gibbs, the Newport lady for whom it was painted, and in 1866 was exposed for sale in the Redwood Library. Two years later it was purchased by Professor S. F. B. Morse, for $ 7,000, and presented to Yale College.

In 1830 the master married again, and his second wife was a cousin of the first, being, like her, a granddaughter of William Ellery, the signer of the Declaration of Independence. Her father was Francis Dana, the Chief Justice of Massachusetts, who married Miss Elizabeth Ellery; and one of her brothers was Richard H. Dana, the poet. She was forty-six years old when Allston married her, and survived him until the year 1862.

CHAPTER V.

A Group of Pictures. — The Valentine, Rosalie, Beatrice, Spalatro, etc. — The 'Belshazzar's Feast.'

MR. ALLSTON painted between forty and fifty pictures in Europe, of which by far the greater number have disappeared. The choicest of his works after returning to America are now preserved in Boston, some in the Museum of Fine Arts, and others in the houses of some of the elder families. A few of these are hereinafter described.

'The Valentine' is a simply colored and composed picture, in which a lady is seen reading a letter, which she holds with both hands. It has been carefully restored, without impairing the merit of the coloring and its charming naturalness. It almost breathes, in the warm life which the skilfully mingled hues simulate, and the delicate gradations of the shadows. Ware says: "I have never been able to invent the terms that would sufficiently express my admiration of that picture. . . . The art can go no further, nor as I believe has it ever gone any further." The model for this picture was Mrs. Russell, a sister of the first Mrs. Allston, a lady whom the artist greatly admired in view of her beautiful character, and whom he represented in several other pictures.

The 'Rosalie' is a graceful and thoughtful woman, sitting in the calm repose of deep contemplation, and twirling the golden chain that falls from her neck, with an exquisitely delicate hand. Ware has called this "one of the most graceful conceptions that artist was ever able to copy upon canvas." George W. Flagg attests that the head of this noble picture was finished in three hours, a marvellous celerity for such a slow and careful artist. She appears to be listening to music, passionate, yet peaceful, as if in the words of the poet-painter's song of 'Rosalie':

> "O, pour upon my soul again
> That sad, unearthly strain,
> That seems from other worlds to plain;
> Thus falling, falling from afar,
> As if some melancholy star
> Had mingled with her light her sighs,
> And dropped them from the skies!

The rapid rise in the price of Allston's pictures after his death is seen in the fact that not long after that sad event $5,000 was offered for the 'Rosalie,' and was refused.

The 'Beatrice' is not unlike the 'Rosalie' in its calm and contemplative air, though its repose is of a deeper and more permanent character. The face is beautiful, being still and self-possessed; and is English rather than Italian in its powerful and transfigured sentiment. Her hair and eyes are soft and brown; her complexion is suffused with tender rosy light; and a strange charm emanates from the radiant face, though it is devoid of physical beauty. Mrs. Jameson calls this picture "most lovely"; Mr. Jarves sees it as "weak and pale"; and Dr. Holmes finds in it "the simple ease of Raphael."

'The Flight of Florimel' is based on an incident in Spenser's "Faerie Queen," showing a dimly lighted forest, without gloom or glare, through which, in the foreground, Florimel is flying on a white horse. Her golden raiment and fair hair form brilliant lights; and her face, backward turned towards the pursuer, is filled with fright and consternation. This exquisite picture was painted for the artist's friend, Loammi Baldwin.

'The Triumphal Song of Miriam on the Destruction of Pharaoh and his Hosts in the Red Sea' is a three-quarter-length figure, with one hand holding the timbrel and the other thrown upward. The picture is filled with exultant life and uplifting joy, and the dramatic effect is powerful in its inspiration. The 'Miriam' was originally bought by David Sears, for $1,000, and is now owned by his son, Frederick R. Sears. Holmes called its coloring Titianesque, and preferred it to any of the master's other pictures, holding it as a link between his scriptural and ideal compositions.

'The Spanish Girl,' one of Allston's most famous works, is notable chiefly for the felicitous art of the landscape background, a dreamy summer scene in the pastoral hill-country of Spain, full of suggestions to the imagination and the soul. The fair lady is sitting on the bank of a lake, which is as calm as a mill-pond, and the warm-tinted Sierra Morena rises beyond. The motive of the scene was set forth by the artist in a sweet poem, wherein Inez awaits by the lake the return of her Isidore from the wars.

'The Death of King John,' though unfinished, was Allston's masterpiece in the expression of emotion in faces, varying from the utter misery of the conscience-stricken sovereign to the deep compassion of the people about his bedside. The design is true and simple, and the composition is complete.

'The Evening Hymn' is a rich and Claude-like picture, in which a ruined Italian castle, by the water-side, is seen in the warm sunset light. On the moss-grown causeway a maiden is sitting, guitar in hand, with her pure and impassioned face upturned to heaven, as if the hymn was already trembling on her lips.

'The Roman Lady' is represented as reading a book which she holds before her. The face is hard and inanimate in its gravity and absorption; but the hands are masterpieces of art, and display the most splendid and natural coloring.

The 'Amy Robsart' was painted for John A. Lowell. It has been suggested that this work illustrates the proverbial inequality of genius, since it shows inferiority both in coloring and in design. On the other hand, Sumner, who saw it while fresh and new, speaks of its beautiful golden hair, "and that sweet look of feeling which you find in all Allston's pictures, particularly of women, — *qualem decet esse sororum.*"

'The Sisters' is a picture of two young girls, in three-quarter size, Titianesque in color, and with the attitude of one of the figures taken from Titian's portrait of his daughter, as Allston frankly stated in the Catalogue.

'The Tuscan Girl' is a fair maiden in a forest, wrapped in meditation, and is described in Allston's poem, beginning, —

> "How pleasant and how sad the turning tide
> Of human life, where side by side
> The child and youth begin to glide
>   Along the vale of years;
> The pure twin-being for a little space,
> With lightsome heart, and yet a graver face,
>   Too young for woe, but not for tears!"

The 'Lorenzo and Jessica' is one of the master's smallest pictures, and one of his most perfect, in the Giorgionesque manner. Therein two lovers are seen sitting side by side, in the hushed and cloudless twilight, gazing together towards the glowing west. Through the deep and now sunken tones of the picture the Italian villa in the background scarcely appears. About the time that this picture was finished the artist was visited by Charles Fraser, his old Carolina friend, and Robert C. Winthrop, to whom he repeated certain verses which he had composed about the subject on which he had been engaged.

The 'Italian Landscape' is a broad and brilliant composition, replete with music and perfume, and overspread with sweet sunshine and poetic repose. It is a far-expanding plain, with a round-arched bridge crossing a still river, a rugged mountain rising majestically in the distance, and a tall stone-pine in the foreground. The 'American Scenery' is a smaller landscape, wrapped in the haze of autumn, with a lonely horseman riding through the rural solitudes. Other poetic phases of nature which Allston illustrated were 'A Sunrise on the Mediterranean,' 'After Sunset,' 'Moonlight,' 'A Forest Scene,' and 'A Mountain Landscape.'

The 'Swiss Landscape' is a grand and shadowy scene, where dark forms appear upon a dim and solitary pathway, near a lake whose waters reflect the stiff pines on the banks and the piles of rugged rocks above. Over all is spread the clear and crystalline atmosphere of the Alps, with stately mountain-forms looming into the sky.

The picture of 'Spalatro's Vision of the Bloody Hand' is founded on a scene in Mrs. Radcliffe's novel of "The Italian," when the monk Schedoni and the assassin Spalatro are advancing through a dark corridor to murder Elena, and Spalatro is suddenly horrified by the apparition of a beckoning bloody hand. He is seen half crouching, as if frozen with intense supernatural fear, and his eyes are dilated with horror; while the undismayed priest stands erect and haughty, holding the lamp above his head, and looking forward into the gloom with clear and steady eye. The picture was but $2\frac{1}{2} \times 1\frac{1}{2}$ feet in size, yet it may well be doubted if any other painting whatever of equal smallness was capable of producing such powerful emotions. Allston justly regarded this as one of his best works; and nowhere else did he show forth so clearly his intense realization of the power of conscience, a feeling which always swayed him with marvellous effect. The picture was burned in 1873, in a mansion on the Hudson.

The 'Spalatro' was painted for Mr. Ball of South Carolina, who chose this from a number of subjects proposed by the artist. Most of the years 1830 and 1831 were spent on this picture, which afterwards for a time graced the Scollay mansion, in Boston. The friends of the master proposed to have it exhibited, for his benefit, since the amount paid for it had been very inadequate to the labor. But he refused to consent to such an exhibition, remarking also: "It was said of Paul Veronese that when he painted for convents he was sometimes paid half in money and half in masses. In like manner I am sometimes content to be paid half in money and part in praises."

One of the most attractive and accessible souvenirs of Allston is the series of certain of his designs, published in Boston soon after his death. This collection includes twenty plates, the largest of which is 20 × 30 inches, from outlines in umber and hasty sketches in chalk. They are full of idealism and refinement, purity and loftiness of conception; and show a profound knowledge of the human form, and the beauty and grace of its best estate. The engravings were skilfully made by the Cheney brothers, and the broad chalk lines were imitated by blending delicate parallel lines. There are six plates from 'Michael Setting the Heavenly Watch,' and four (of angels) from 'Jacob's Dream.' Others represent 'Uriel in the Sun,' 'A Sibyl,' 'Heliodorus,' 'Prometheus,' 'The Prodigal Son,' 'Dido and Æneas,' and a ship in a gale at sea. The latter was probably taken from the sketch of which Mrs. Jameson said, "It was a sea-piece, — a thunder-storm retiring, and a frigate bending to the gale; it was merely a sketch in white chalk upon a red ground, and about five feet high, as nearly as I can recollect, — not even the dead coloring was laid on; I never saw such an effect produced by such a vehicle, and had not mine own eyes seen it, I could not have conceived or believed it possible. There was absolute motion in the clouds and waves, — all the poetry, all the tumult of the tempest were there! — and, I repeat, it was a sketch in white chalk, — not even a shadow!" Another design in the book was the 'Fairies on the Seashore,' a graceful fancy, with a column of fairies rising from the sea-washed strand into the bright sky. Mr. W. H. Prescott sent a copy of this work to Lord Morpeth, praising it highly, and quoting Allston's poetry freely.

The 'Belshazzar's Feast' took form in the artist's mind as early as April, 1817, as appears in his letter of that date to Irving: "One of these subjects (and the most important) is the large picture, — the prophet Daniel interpreting the handwriting on the wall before Belshazzar. I have made a highly finished sketch of it. I think the composition the best I have ever made. It contains a multitude of figures, and (if I may be allowed to say so) they are without confusion. Don't you think it a fine subject? I know not any that so happily unites the magnificent and the awful. A mighty sovereign, surrounded by his whole court, intoxicated with his own state, in the midst of his revelry palsied in a moment, under the spell of a preternatural hand suddenly tracing his doom on the wall before him; his powerless limbs, like a wounded spider's, shrunk up to his body, while his heart, compressed to a point, is only kept from vanishing by the terrific suspense that animates it during the interpretation of his mysterious sentence. His less guilty but scarcely less agitated queen, the panic-struck courtiers and concubines, the splendid and deserted banquet-table, the half-arrogant, half-astounded magicians, the holy vessels of the temple (shining as it were in triumph through the gloom), and the calm, solemn contrast of the prophet, standing, like an animated pillar, in the midst, breathing forth the oracular destruction of the empire!"

The sketch alluded to is now in the possession of Mr. Richard H. Dana, who also has the sketch of 'Christ Healing the Sick,' a powerful one of the head of Jeremiah, a portrait of Coleridge, a large landscape, and several other unfinished works of his famous kinsman.

The great painting of 'Belshazzar's Feast' was begun in England, before 1818, on a canvas 16×12 feet in size. When the artist returned to America, he said of it: "All the laborious part is over, but there still remains about six or eight months' more work to do to it." He little dreamed that the twenty-five remaining years of his life would not avail to finish it, and that sixty years later it would be hung in the Boston Museum of Fine Arts, still incomplete, though glorious. This great composition was valued at $10,000, held by several wealthy patrons in ten shares, of which a certain percentage was paid in advance. It must have been some unpleasant experiences in this matter which led him to advise Sully, "O, do not undertake anything that cannot be accomplished by your own means."

Immediately on his return from England Allston unrolled the almost finished picture, and submitted it to the honest severity of Stuart's criticism. That great painter pointed out certain radical errors in the work, which its author acknowledged, and had perhaps foreseen; and Allston thereupon began the immense task of reconstructing the entire design. He was obliged to devote many weeks to changing the perspective, during which he made more than twenty thousand chalk-lines in circles and arcs, to bring the amended figures into correct drawing. The operations of laying in the ground-colors and finishing them with the glazing colors followed, involving more labor than the painting of a new picture on a fresh canvas would have cost, besides the terrible mental strain and distress which necessarily ensued. Stuart told Dr. Channing, at the beginning, that it would never be finished, because of "the rapid growth of the artist's mind, so that the work of this month or year was felt to be imperfect the next, under the better knowledge of more time, and must be done over again, or greatly altered, and, therefore, could never come to an end." But this opinion seems unwarranted, and had the great master's life been spared a little longer he would doubtless have linked the name of the Assyrian king with the noblest achievement of American art. Charles Sumner thought that if Allston's last illness had been a lingering one, he would have ordered the destruction of the unfinished picture.

Martin's famous picture of 'Belshazzar's Feast' was exhibited in London in 1821, and Allston wrote to its author that he "would not mind a walk of ten miles, over a quickset hedge, before breakfast, to see it." Martin said: "This is something, from a bad walker and a worse riser." The subject had been suggested to him by Allston, who held a conception of its proper composition totally different from his own, and the two artists had a prolonged discussion on the question. Allston suggested that Martin's conception was well set forth in a prize poem at Cambridge, written by T. S. Hughes, which the English painter afterwards read, and then determined to paint the picture. Leslie and other friends endeavored to dissuade him from his proposed treatment of the subject, but in vain. It is said that he borrowed Allston's idea of making the light in the picture proceed from the miraculous inscription, and that Allston abandoned his own version upon hearing of this plagiarism.

In 1823 Allston showed to Chester Harding and Jonathan Mason the great picture in his studio. It was all finished then, except the single figure of Daniel, and Allston told his visitors to see Leslie when they reached England, and describe the work to him, but to allow no one else to hear of it.

When Harding went to Washington, in the winter of 1828, he gave Allston the use of his spacious studio, wherein to finish the 'Belshazzar's Feast': " He painted all winter, instead, on a landscape; and when I came home, I found he had wiped out his winter's work, saying it was not worthy of him. He smoked incessantly, became nervous, and was haunted by fears that his great picture would not come up to the standard of his high reputation. One day he went to his friend Loammi Baldwin, and said, 'I have to-day blotted out my four years' work on my 'Handwriting on the Wall.'"

The delay in completing this immense composition' was a circumstance which sorely troubled the artist for years, and called forth many annoying inquiries from the public, if not from the subscribers to the picture. But while thus vexed by worldly cares and responsibilities, he was unable to consecrate his time to the great work, and therefore it remained unfinished. He wrote: "Indeed, I have *already* bestowed upon it as much mental and manual labor as, under another state of mind, would have completed several such pictures. But to go into the subject of all the obstacles and the hindrances upon my spirit would hardly be consistent with delicacy and self-respect." The public had formed exaggerated ideas of the new picture, in view of the artist's well-known genius and prolonged seclusion, and Allston was alarmed by the general prediction that the 'Belshazzar's Feast' was destined to be one of the most brilliant triumphs of American art.

Some of his friends had stood as models and others had heard him describe his conception of the proper treatment of the theme; and from these glowing accounts had been scattered abroad, and the public was in an expectant attitude. The dreary consciousness of pecuniary embarrassments, the lack of proper models and other properties, and the delicate health of the artist combined to persuade him, from time to time, that he had undertaken a task too great for his means and strength, and caused him to put it aside in discouragement and dissatisfaction. Thus, frequently abandoned and as often renewed, the work went on slowly for a quarter of a century, and was finally left unfinished, a mere fragment, yet the delight of later generations. He was at work on this picture less than seven hours before he died.

The amount of labor freely lavished on the 'Belshazzar's Feast' was enormous, and for years the slight and feeble figure of the artist moved up the ladders and along the stagings before the great canvas, laden with the house-painter's brushes which put on the priming coats, and then going through the prolonged toils of finishing the work in its details. Most of this should have been done by pupils, but of such there were none, and the task was devolved all too heavily, in summer's heat and winter's frost, on one weary pair of hands. The architecture and objects of still-life in the picture are worked up with infinite labor, and wasted many golden days. The unnatural and elongated human figures which still remain unchanged and unfinished show the direction of the artist's labors, and their exceeding complexity and magnitude.

Perhaps he was led into the pursuit of conceptions alien to his nature by the overmastering power with which the scene of the fifth chapter of Daniel seized and excited him, in its artistic potentialities. It may be, also, that he yielded to the mania of British artists, in his time, for painting huge canvases in the "grand style," as West, Barry, and others had done. But the vast works of Tintoretto were as far removed from his manifestation of genius as the achievements of the skilful stone-carver are from those of the lapidary, — and for this great and stately, but incomplete and unsatisfactory, ruin of art and imagination, America has had to pay too dearly, in the loss of many a delicate and highly polished jewel of painting which might otherwise have been hers.

In this great composition Allston attempted to accomplish something to which his genius was unsuited, though it was fully equal to it. Imagination, mental force, religious fervor, — all these he had in sufficient degree, but his preference was for another kind of subject, and his monastic spirit chose to pour itself more richly into simpler subjects. In life he disliked crowds and any manner of bustling confusion, and so also in art he chose quiet scenes, of simple elements, single figures, or solitary landscapes, and into these he put himself with abundant faith and sympathy. How different was the conception of his vast illumination of the Assyrian drama!

The scene represented is that sublime event which is described in the fifth chapter of Daniel, when "Belshazzar the king made a great feast to a thousand of his lords, and drank wine before the thousand"; and while he and his princes and concubines are drinking from the golden vessels plundered from the temple of Jehovah at Jerusalem, a hand appears, writing on the wall of the palace. The terrified king and his soothsayers cannot read the inscription, and Daniel, "in whom is the spirit of the holy gods," is summoned, and interprets it as a prediction of the speedy fall of the kingdom. The scene shows the great palace-hall, with the enthroned king, and the queen and her attendants, the foreground being occupied by Daniel and the astrologers, the middle distance by the feasters around their table, and the remote background by the vast interior of a temple, with the idol thereof under a blazing circle of lights, and people hurrying up the broad steps in terror.

The king's face is devoid of obvious and caricatured terror, but his whole form seems to be cramped and frozen by unspeakable awe, — at least, so the artist strove to represent it. The form of Daniel is good, but the face is not endowed with striking power, — nor does it represent Daniel Webster, as the gossips of those days said that it would. The minor groups show some faces convulsed with terror and others absolutely unmoved and apparently without fear, concerning which it is easier to believe that the artist's design is not yet fully understood than that he has laboriously portrayed an absurdity, or avoided a theatrical vulgarity by introducing an abnormal apathy. The grandest face in the picture is that of the queen, full of regal beauty and pride, scornful and contemptuous, towering in heroic self-dependence beside the sinking king, yet holding her attendant's hand for support. Her costume is magnificent, and was perfectly and delicately finished.

The architecture of the palace-hall is marked by rows of small columns, which Ware calls a fatal blemish on the picture, as producing an effect of littleness and meanness quite inadmissible in Assyrian buildings, and foreign to grandeur and sublimity. The dimly seen and towering pillars of the idol's temple, with its countless stairs, and the mysterious god, wrapped in a wonderful atmosphere of distance, are set in the strongest contrast, and exhibit a triumphant excellence.

The grand and crowning excellence of the picture is in its wealth of gorgeous Venetian coloring, pure and harmonious, and in all parts resplendent. The most notable points, in this regard, are the figure of the queen, Daniel's head, the malignant astrologer who looks out of the picture, and the group of Jews in the centre. The latter, though in the shadow, is finished with the most exquisite delicacy and perfection, and appears almost self-luminous. The harmony of the entire composition seems the product of a single day of inspired labor, when the great thought at once took faultless form, rather than the toilsome and oft-abandoned drudgery of twenty-five years.

An eminent and competent critic has said that if this picture had been finished "it would have gone near to eclipse all that had gone before it," claiming for it not only sublimity of conception and richness of coloring, but also a rare minuteness of finish throughout the work, "which, though so large, completed, would have had at once all the truth and delicacy of a cabinet gem, and the breadth and grandeur which belong to colossal subjects; which is just the truth of Nature, whose works, though ever so large, are never finished with any the less minuteness and perfection."

CHAPTER VI.

The Studio at Cambridgeport. — Lowell's Pen-Sketch. — Mrs. Jameson. — The Exhibition. — Eminent Friends. — The Death of Allston.

EARLY in 1831 Allston established himself in a new painting-room, which he had built at Cambridgeport, in which village he also made his home. His former studio in Boston was converted into a livery stable, and after that event he had painted in a small chamber. The 'Belshazzar's Feast' had been rolled up and put away in a packing-case for three years, for the artist had constant need of money, and must needs paint small pictures to earn it. But he said, at this time, that if he ever became free from his debts and the pressing demands of daily existence, he should devote the remainder of his life to large paintings. In a letter to McMurtrie he wrote: "I have been married about a year, and this village is now my home. It is but two miles from Boston, where I can be at any time, by means of an hourly stage, in twenty minutes. I am in better health, and certainly in better spirits, than I have been these ten years."

He chose to settle in Cambridgeport on account of its close vicinity both to Boston and to Harvard College, within easy walk of his friends at either place. He needed a large quantity of land for the new house and studio, and could get it in that village at slight expense. As to the unattractiveness of Cambridgeport as a place of residence he cared but little, since he was not affected by outside surroundings. In all Cambridge there were but 6,000 inhabitants at this time. The greater part of what is now Cambridgeport was then (in the native dialect) a *huckleberry pastur*. Woods were not wanting on its outskirts, of pine and oak and maple, and the rarer tupelo with downward limbs. Allston's house was at the corner of Magazine and Auburn Streets; and the studio was hard by, in the rear of the Baptist Church of the village, having but one door, and that on the side away from the street, opening on a path which led across the garden to the artist's house. There were several small trees and bits of shrubbery between the two buildings, and the studio door was enarched with climbing vines. The painting-room had but a single window, which opened toward the garden, and was very long and high. The children of the vicinity had many a ghostly theory about this lone studio of New England. Within, the room was surrounded by cabinets, whose doors bore many a rude sketch and inscription.

Mrs. Allston's means were not small, and hence the dreamy artist was free from the desolating apprehensions of want and poverty.

The Shepard Congregational Society was formed in 1829, when the old First Parish in Cambridge became Unitarian. In 1830-31 the new society built a meeting-house, partly from plans furnished by Allston, who used to lead out his friends and visitors at evening to a point about a third of a mile southeast of the building, and bid them to admire it, repeating the lines: —

> "If thou wouldst view fair Melrose aright,
> Go visit it by the pale moonlight."

After leaving Boston, Allston usually attended this church, with which his wife and her family were closely connected, finding there as strong a defence of Trinitarianism as in his own Episcopal Church. On saints' days and other high ecclesiastical festivals he used to attend service at St. Paul's, in Boston. He was fond of reading the Bible and the works of the old Anglican divines, and once wrote a long and able essay on Christianity as supplying an inherent want of human nature.

Let us read James Russell Lowell's exquisite pen-sketch of our Allston: " So refined was his whole appearance, so fastidiously neat his apparel, — but with a neatness that seemed less the result of care and plan than a something as proper to the man as whiteness to the lily, — that you would have at once classed him with those individuals, rarer than great captains and almost as rare as great poets, whom Nature sends into the world to fill the arduous office of Gentleman. ... A *nimbus* of hair, fine as an infant's, and early white, showing refinement of organization and the predominance of the spiritual over the physical, undulated and floated around a face that seemed like pale flame, and over which the flitting shades of expression chased each other,

fugitive and gleaming as waves upon a field of rye. It was a countenance that, without any beauty of feature, was very beautiful. I have said that it looked like pale flame, and can find no other words for the impression it gave. Here was a man all soul, whose body seemed a lump of finest clay, whose service was to feed with magic oils, rare and fragrant, that wavering fire which hovered over it. You, who are an adept in such matters, would have detected in the eyes that artist-look which seems to see pictures ever in the air, and which, if it fall on you, makes you feel as if all the world were a gallery, and you yourself the rather indifferent Portrait of a Gentleman hung therein.

"Allston carried thither [to Italy] a nature open on the southern side, and brought it back so steeped in rich Italian sunshine that the east winds (whether physical or intellectual) of Boston and the dusts of Cambridgeport assailed it in vain. To that bare wooden studio one might go to breathe Venetian air, and, better yet, the very spirit wherein the elder brothers of Art labored, etherealized by metaphysical speculation and sublimed by religious fervor. The beautiful old man! Here was genius with no volcanic explosions (the mechanical result of vulgar gunpowder often), but lovely as a Lapland night; here was fame, not sought after nor worn in any cheap French fashion as a ribbon at the button-hole, but so gentle, so retiring, that it seemed no more than an armored and emboldened modesty; here was ambition, undebased by rivalry and incapable of the sidelong look; and all these massed and harmonized together into a purity and depth of character, into a *tone*, which made the daily life of the man the greatest masterpiece of the artist."

Allston's life at Cambridgeport was one of great seclusion, as became a scholar, an artist, and an invalid. He had a small but choice circle of friends, including his kindred and a few intellectual companions, and frequently welcomed artists and travellers to his studio. But the hospitalities of the great families of Boston and Cambridge, though freely offered to him, were generally declined, since he preferred to devote his life to nobler pursuits than those of mere social pleasure. His high religious concentration and reverent consecration to the true and the beautiful attracted to him the noblest minds of New England, as they had previously drawn the gentle Malbone, the philosophic Coleridge, and the cultured Irving. He won the admiration and homage of the choicest men and women of his age and race; and passed through life with an earnest love for his fellows and a fearless faith in God.

Mrs. Jameson visited Allston in Cambridgeport, and said that the New Englanders "triumphed in the astonishment and admiration of a stranger who started to find Venetian sentiment, grandeur, and color in the works of a Boston painter, buried out of sight, almost out of mind, for five-and-twenty years,—a whole generation of European amateurs. . . . He was an admirable narrator, his good stories being often invented for the occasion. The vivacity of his conceptions, and the glowing language in which he could clothe them, rendered his conversation inexpressibly delightful and exciting. I remember, after an evening spent with him, returning home very, very late (I think it was near three in the morning), with the feelings of one who had been magnetized." Such was still his custom, to spend a great part of the night in conversation, and then to rise very late. Miss Clarke once informed him that she was engaged in painting a sunrise scene, and rose early in order to see the sun when it passed above the horizon. "How *does* it look?" asked he, in perfect good faith.

In 1835 Allston's time was so thoroughly engaged that he was obliged to decline several commissions, and wrote to Hayward stating that he had engagements on hand which would occupy him for over two years in advance. The wealthy citizens of Boston were unsparing in their liberality towards him, whom they admired as much as a man as they respected as an artist.

Soon afterwards the master wrote: "I had a delightful visit from Morse. Its only fault was being too short. The same from my old friend Fraser." Morse, the President of the National Academy, on returning from this journey, exclaimed: "I go to Allston as a comet goes to the sun, not to add to his material, but to imbibe light from him." Morse found his old master delightfully situated at Cambridge, engrossed by congenial studies and assiduous labors, and prophesied that the 'Michael setting the Guard of the Heavenly Host at the Gates of Paradise,' and other pictures then under way, would rank him by the side of Raphael. In 1834 Dunlap — shall we not call him the American Vasari? — placed Allston at the head of living artists.

When the Government was arranging the decoration of the Rotunda in the Capitol, Allston was commissioned to paint the great pictures for the panels. He, however, declined this flattering appointment, and urged the fitness of Morse, his old pupil, then President of the National Academy of Design. But John Quincy Adams introduced a resolution in Congress in favor of foreign artists, alleging that there were no American painters competent to the work; and Fenimore Cooper answered him with a severe and masterly paper in the New York *Evening Post*. This reply was attributed to Morse, whose name was therefore rejected by the committee; and Allston hastened to offer his sympathy and consolation. When the master was consulted, some years before, as to his willingness to paint pictures for the Rotunda, he had replied: "I will undertake one only, and I choose my own subject. No battle-piece." He often avowed his disinclination to paint battle scenes, — Charles Sumner has borne witness to it, and who then can doubt?

Allston united with Cooper and Everett in securing for Greenough the Government commission for the statue of Washington, which resulted in the noble work now in the Capitol Park at Washington. In later years he joined Sumner in aiding Greenough and Crawford; and on the very evening of his death he talked enthusiastically of Crawford and his works. He was also very friendly to G. P. A. Healy, who gave the master one of his skilful copies after Titian.

In 1838 Allston frequently visited Harding's, where he met N. P. Willis, then a handsome and poetic young man, with a free and sparkling pen. When these two skilful story-tellers met, the winged hours flew rapidly by, and brought the midnight full soon. About this same time Wordsworth inquired earnestly of Charles Sumner about the welfare of Allston, whom he "regarded as the first artist of the age, and was attached to by twofold relations, — first, as his own friend, and then as the affectionate friend of Coleridge." Ticknor wrote home to Dana, "There is not a man in Europe who can paint a picture like Allston." Giulian C. Verplanck characterized the artist as *Arte clarus, literis ornatus, moribus pulchrior*.

Allston's chief pupil while at Cambridge was Miss Sarah Clarke, the sister of James Freeman Clarke, and now a resident of Rome. She was an intimate friend of Margaret Fuller, who once said of her: "Her neighborhood casts the mildness and purity too of the moonbeam on the else party-colored scene."

To a young man who asked his advice about becoming an artist, he said: "It is a calling full of delays and disappointments, and I can never recommend any one to pursue it. If he *must* be a painter, let him come prepared to bear up a mighty burden." He advised a young artist thus: "Do not be anxious, but put faith in your fingers. When I paint, I often do not look at my palette; I take off my colors by a secret sympathy between my hand and the pigments." Another tyro in art submitted a landscape for the master's criticism, and he remarked, "Your trees do not look as if the birds could fly through them." When some one asked him if a certain picture of his own was not his favorite, he rejoined, "I love *all* my children."

In 1839 an exhibition of forty-two of Allston's pictures was held in Harding's Gallery, in Boston; and although his larger works were not included, yet the beauty and exquisite finish of those displayed created a profound impression on all appreciative spectators. The originality and versatility of these works attested the wide range of his conceptions, as well as the individuality of his genius; and American art for the first time could display, in one group and from one master-hand, the choicest excellences of painting and design, thoroughly harmonious in their perfect finish, noble conceptions, and permanent power. The artist himself was enraptured to see once more the works of twoscore years, many of which had been out of his sight ever since they had left the studio.

Tuckerman has described this exhibition as follows: "We turned from the impressive figure of the 'Reviving Dead,' slowly renewing vitality at the touch of the prophet's bones, to the pensive beauty of 'Beatrice,' ineffably lovely and sad; the countenance of 'Rosalie' seemed kindled like that of the maiden described by Wordsworth, as if music 'born of murmuring sound had passed into her face'; aerial in her movement, and embodied grace in her attitude and drapery, 'Miriam' sounded the timbrel; the very foot of the scribe appeared to listen to Jeremiah, — stern, venerable, and prophetic; keenly glittered the Alpine summits, and sweetly fell the moonbeams, and darkly rose the forests in the landscapes, as if glimpses of real nature, instead of their reflex, made alive the canvas; full of character and dignity were the portraits; magnificent old Jews' heads, and exquisite brows of maidens, and imposing forms of prophets, and marvellous light and shade, deep, lucent, mellow hues, — all flitted before the senses of the visitor, while each picture formed an inexhaustible object of contemplation, and became a permanently beautiful and impressive reminiscence."

Margaret Fuller wrote a long article for "The Dial," criticising the pictures in the Allston Exhibition, and reflecting severely on the historical compositions. The Dead Man was an offensive subject; the Massacre of the Innocents had no force; Jeremiah was a robust and angry Jew; Miriam was shallow-eyed and inadequate; and the Witch of Endor was attended by a stage-ghost and a degraded king. Therefore, as Miss Fuller reasoned, Allston was not adapted to historic works, but to the exposition of Beauty, in which he showed rare subjective excellence, bland delicacy, perfect equipoise, and unconscious self-possession, with great skill in drapery and an exquisite sensibility to color. In "The Dial" for 1840 there was a long poem, contrasting the Italian landscapes of Gaspar Poussin, Domenichino, and Allston.

Mr. Spear, the historical painter, a friend of Allston's, states that about 1840 Allston told him that Correggio was the master on whose works he had modelled his style. He extolled the "mottled" manner, and explained his own custom of painting with blue, red, and yellow mingled, taking the color which he wished to be predominant as the last upon the brush, and carefully stippling over the work. He repeatedly advised Spear to "paint in the family of the *ishes*," that is, to avoid sharp and pronounced colors, and to prefer reddish to red, bluish to blue, etc.

Harding's first portrait of Allston represented him in his favorite blue coat with brass buttons and buff waistcoat. One arm is placed akimbo with such a martial air that the friends of the sitter afterwards playfully entitled him "Colonel Allston." About the year 1845 Harding painted from memory an admirable portrait of Allston, which was purchased by Mr. Batchelder a few years later, and still remains in his mansion at Cambridge.

Sumner visited the studio in 1840, and reported that Allston had unrolled the 'Belshazzar's Feast' across one entire side-wall, but had carefully curtained it from view. It was during the year 1840 that he painted 'The Bride.'

Allston was a great friend of George Ticknor, and delighted to visit his famous library. In 1841 Mr. Ticknor wrote of a dinner at which Longfellow, Prescott, Hillard, and Allston were present with him. The artist was a frequent visitor at the mansion of Professor Norton, in Cambridge, where some of his minor pictures are still preserved.

In 1841 Wordsworth wrote from Rydal Mount to Professor Reed of Philadelphia, telling how many years ago he had been introduced to the master by "our common friend Coleridge, who had seen much of Mr. Allston when they were both living at Rome." After Wordsworth had been apprized, by the Rev. Mr. Waterston, of the death of the artist at Cambridge, he wrote lamenting "the death of that admirable artist and amiable man, my old friend Mr. Allston."

When Lord Morpeth (the Earl of Carlisle) visited Boston, in 1841, he was introduced to Story, Channing, Longfellow, Bancroft, Ticknor, Emerson, and Prescott. Sumner also made him acquainted with Allston. At this time Greenough was urging Allston to come to Italy, and received a letter from Sumner, telling how Longfellow and himself had recently drawn out an evening's visit at the artist's until midnight. He added that Allston was then busily engaged on the 'Belshazzar's Feast,' and would allow no one to enter the studio.

In his American Notes, Dickens says that "Washington Allston, the painter (who wrote 'Monaldi'), is a fine specimen of a glorious old genius." Grattan, in his "Civilized America," calls Allston "the foremost of American painters."

Griswold says of the master, "Not long before his death I dined with him, and was astonished when a companion intimated that it was after midnight. We had listened six or seven hours without a thought of the lapse of time. His manners were gentle and dignified. His dress was simple and old-fashioned, — a blue coat with plain bright buttons, a buff vest, and drab pantaloons. His face was thin and serious, with remarkably expressive eyes; his hair, fine, long, and silvery white, fell gracefully upon his shoulders ; and his voice was soft, earnest, and musical."

Allston read his lectures on art to Professors Longfellow and Felton, during the last winter of his life, and the latter thus describes the scene: "It was a most interesting and impressive thing to hear that beloved and venerated person, after making all his peculiar arrangements, — placing his lights each in a certain position, — setting his footstool between his chair and the fire, warming his feet, — lighting his cigar, and reducing his manuscripts to order, — read on, hour after hour, those masterly expositions clothed in the richest forms of language ; . . . his large, mysterious eye growing larger with the interest of his subject, his voice increasing in volume and strength, his pale countenance transfigured by his kindling soul to an almost supernatural expression, until, as he uttered passage after passage of harmonious and magnificent discourse, he seemed to become the inspired prophet, declaring a new revelation of the religion of art. . . . Mr. Allston's conversation was singularly attractive. The Graces, seeking a shrine, certainly chose his soul for their temple. His peculiar and striking personal appearance can never be forgotten. His tall and slender figure, his pale countenance, the towering pile of his forehead, his regular and pleasing features, his large hazel eye, the venerable locks that waved in the solemn beauty of silvered age from his shapely head, formed in their combination an image which he who has once seen sees forever. His manners were mild, sincere, urbane, and warm, expressing all the blended softness, grace, and dignity of his character. His voice was the gentlest utterance that ever mortal spoke in."

Not many days before he died Allston received a visit from his old friend, the Rev. R. C. Waterston, who bore him an invitation from Weir to make a visit to the latter's residence at West Point. He expressed a strong desire to accept this pleasant courtesy, but said that he was too busy at painting; and added, stretching forth his arms, "My wrists are so tired every night that they absolutely *ache*."

The closing scenes of Allston's life cannot be better described than in the words of the venerable poet, Richard H. Dana, in his letter to Professor Morse: "Your old friend, and one who spoke of you with deep affection, was taken from us most suddenly, and I may say most unexpectedly; for, though he seemed to be failing fast, his friends had no suspicion of a disease of the organs that would take him away instantly. The great arteries were not essentially impaired; but one or two that fed the heart itself were ossified. While none of the intestinal organs could be said to be in a healthy state, none, with the exception of those I have mentioned as being ossified, were in so diseased a condition that he might not have lived some years longer. So long ago as when —— took a bust of him his friends thought he would not live long, but he recruited. The winter before last he was severely ill, and we feared for him then. From that attack he but partially recovered, and from that time was plainly, with short terms of a better state, a broken-down, failing man. His strength was not sufficient for his labor; and, while his intellect was as clear as ever, it was evident that the servant, the body, was too much weakened to do its appointed work. He spoke of himself as an old, broken-down man. It was plain, his wife says, from the dreadful depression he was under for the last ten months, when his friends were not around him, that he was suffering under the apprehension that he should not have strength to finish what he was about. God, in His mercy, spared him from living on with this thought to prey on him, and took him away in a moment, but with a touch as gentle as the breaking morning light. Both my sisters and my daughter were there, preparatory to leaving him for the summer. All but my daughter went to bed. She sat talking to him. He was strongly attached to her; and had spoken of her most affectionately, as he was wont to do, the last time I saw him. 'I like to talk to her, for she always takes my meaning at once,' he said to me. He said many kind things to her this last night. 'You are my niece,' said he. 'You are more to me, — you are my child. There are relations nearer than those of blood.' Twice he put his arms gently round her, and the second time kissed her forehead, and then lowered his head for her to kiss his cheek. He then looked upward, and his eyes were as if he was seeing into the world of holiness and all peace, and he said, 'I want you to be perfect, perfect. . . . I do not feel like talking,' he soon added, sat down, drew a chair to him for her to sit by him, took her hand, and occasionally spoke in somewhat the same strain. Between twelve and one o'clock he complained of a pain in the chest; he had felt the same once before, about three weeks previous to this. She advised his taking something for it, not thinking of it, however, as anything of much importance; so that, when he went up to his wife's chamber to get what she recommended, she herself went off to bed. He moved about as usual, and when his wife offered to go down and prepare something, he answered, 'O, no! I can do it just as well myself.' He went down again. She stopped to get something which she thought he might want, and followed him in five minutes. She found him sitting in his usual place, with his writing apparatus, which he had just taken out, near him, his feet on the hearth, and his head resting on the back of his chair, in just the position in which he often took his nap. She went up to him; his eyes were open, and, from their appearance, she thought he might have fainted. They were all instantly with him. One of my sisters said to him, 'Mr. Allston, we are all here.' His eyes soon closed. A physician was called, they, in the mean time, doing all they could to revive him. There is very little doubt that life had stopped when his wife reached him. His physician says that he must have gone without a moment's pain, — that it was a mere closing.

"So beautiful an expression as was on his face, as he lay sleeping in Jesus, I never saw on the face of man. Spirits were with his spirit. And a most humble being he was before his God. In Christ and the great Atonement was his only trust. Trust, do I say? it was his realized, fervid life. Not a fortnight before his death he opened his whole soul to the clergyman here, — a most interesting man, — who told me that such childlike, undoubting faith it was delightful to sit and hear poured forth. . . . I wish you could have seen more of Allston, particularly within the last year of his life.... If ever *heavenly-mindedness* showed itself in its *life* and *beauty*, it made itself visible to the mind of Allston, — humble, childlike, himself nothing, Christ all things, — love overflowed him, and the harmony of the upper world pervaded him, and harmonized for him all nature and all art. These were not separated from his religious life, because they were taken up into it and sanctified and made beautiful."

While Clevenger was making Allston's bust the master was suffering under almost continual pain in the face, with a resulting expression of distress and rigidity of muscles. But after his decease Brackett took a cast from his face, whereof Dana said: "So beautiful was the countenance after death, so softened the muscles, and rounded and smoothed the face, that he looked as he did years back, before disease and distress of mind had so preyed upon him." Four years later Allston's head was modelled by Paul Duggan, for a medal struck by the American Art Union.

Professor Morse, who had always sustained an almost filial relation to Allston, hastened from Washington to Cambridge to pay the last honors to his departed master. He secured as a precious memento a brush with which he was painting the day he died, still moist with the paint which he had been laying on 'The Feast of Belshazzar.' This relic was presented by Morse to the National Academy of Design, where it is still carefully preserved.

Richard H. Dana and Christopher P. Cranch wrote obituary poems on Allston. Dr. Albro, the pastor of the Shepard Congregational Society, delivered a long and appreciative sermon on his illustrious parishioner, which was afterwards printed and circulated. Albro applied to the deceased artist the words of Jeremy Taylor about the Countess of Carberry: "As if she knew nothing of it, she had a low opinion of herself; and, like a fair taper, she shined to all the room; yet round about her own station she cast a shadow and a cloud, and so shined to everybody but herself."

Many relics of Allston are preserved with pious care in Boston and Cambridge. Mr. Richard H. Dana, Jr., has his favorite chair, the last quill-pen and painting-brush which he used, the tortoise-shell tobacco-box which Collins gave him, the plate on which he mixed his colors the day he died, and other rare mementoes. In 1863 Miss Judkins presented to the Massachusetts Historical Society his blender for mingling colors.

Allston's remains were placed in the old Dana tomb, in the churchyard opposite Harvard College, where they still remain. The tomb is subterranean, and has no mark by which it can be recognized. The funeral was an impressive ceremony, having occurred just after dark, when the white moonlight streamed on the statuesque face of the dead master, and the burial service was read by the light of lanterns. Sumner, Story, and other eminent men were present at the grave. The first interment in this venerable cemetery occurred before the year 1650, and many professors of the college and venerable scholars have been buried there. Among the solemn graves are the tombs of the Vassals, the Belchers, and other high families of the colonial era. Sumner endeavored to raise $ 2,000 for a monument to Allston at Mount Auburn; but the movement failed, on account of Mrs. Allston's opposition. Some memorial should be raised, however humble and plain, over the Dana tomb, in order that the pilgrim of art may find the grave of the American Titian.

CHAPTER VII.

Allston as an Author. — "The Sylphs." — "The Two Painters."
— Minor Poems. — "Monaldi." — "Lectures on Art." — Studio
Aphorisms.

In literature Allston exemplified his wide culture by meritorious works as a poet, novelist, essayist, metaphysician, and critic. He would have made as great a success in letters as in art, if he had devoted the same energy to the pen as to the pencil.

The volume of poems published in London, and republished in Boston, proves that the Cambridge master had a high degree of inspiration in that direction; and well-nigh takes rank with the sonnets of Michael Angelo and the satires of Salvator Rosa. The poems are light, sprightly, and gentle, full of particularity and truth, and showing a fine appreciation of nature and a lively imagination. They do not stir the intenser passions, nor open up realms of mystery or excitement, but rest in the fair sunlight, amid the delicate perfume of nature, placid and peaceful, and perceiving, with the eyes of the spirit of love, the beauty of the world beneath its outer incrustations of vice and hatred. Sometimes the innocent muse ascends to inspiring realms of joyous magnificence, in the dominion of the imagination, and sometimes flickering flashes of playful satire play through the else shadowy passages. Such poems as "Rosalie" and "The Tuscan Girl" illustrate his paintings in the most exquisite manner, showing the individuality of the artist and the purity of the man, and marking the unity whereby genius harmonizes all expressions to a common principle.

The first poem in the book is "The Sylphs of the Seasons," containing sixty-nine stanzas, and with minute felicity and deep introspection illustrating the effects of the scenery of the seasons on the human mind. The poet first has a vision of a desert cave, and then is carried in dream to a lofty castle, looking down on a plain adorned with scenery of every period, and with a double throne in its great hall. Four fairies, representing the seasons, are grouped there, and inform the poet that the throne is his, and he is to choose one of them to share it with him. Each of them sings to him of her charms of person and mind, beginning with Spring, who speaks of her cheerful influences on humanity.

> "And next the Sylph of Summer fair;
> The while her crispéd, golden hair
> Half veiled her sunny eyes,"

derides the chilling fogs of Spring, and bids the poet consider how her sweet languors, her rich scenery, and her visionary nights had "made the body's indolence the vigor of the mind."

> "And now, in accents deep and low,
> Like voice of fondly cherished woe,
> The Sylph of Autumn sad,"

declining to boast of her bright-hued fruits and golden harvests and rainbow forests, bids the poet consider how her falling leaves and stormy seas and lurid sunsets taught him to muse on the decay of earthly pleasures, the melancholy advance of Death, and the sublimity of the life immortal. Last comes the Sylph of Winter, with piercing voice, vaunting the majestic and heart-stirring influences of her wild tempests, when from "Old Hecla's cloudy height thou"

> "Hast known my petrifying wind
> Wild ocean's curling billows bind,
> Like bending sheaves by harvest hind,
> Erect in icy death."

She sings of Nature sleeping under her robes of snowy plains, enriched by sunset with countless colors; of the exquisite beauty of her frost-work; and the refining and ennobling memories and images, free from sensuousness, which arose in her long and solemn nights.

The poet stood "all motionless and mute," unable to choose between such multifarious and seductive charms, until the break of day, when he awoke under the light of a new sun. Some of the descriptive passages are of the most finished and exquisite beauty and delicacy, and reveal the earnest working of a most sensitive and creative imagination.

"The Two Painters" is a metric satire of six hundred and forty lines, which Dana says "in easy and narrative style reminds us of the tales of Swift, Prior, and Gay." It is in ridicule of the idea that artistic excellence in one department alone, scorning the others, can reach perfection.

> "Once on a time in Charon's wherry,
> Two Painters met, on Styx's ferry,"

the one a *colorist*, and the other a painter of *mind*, and wrangled so noisily that the grim boatman silenced them as "unmannered ghosts." Deep-whizzing through the wave, amid the desolate cries of low-crouching spectre-birds, the sheeted dead passed onward through the gloom, and met the social shades of many other inquisitive ghosts upon the further strand. Poets, painters, politicians, philosophers, and other whilom great ones gathered round to ask how the world still regarded their memories; but they were hurried to the judgment-seat of Minos, who chose the spirit of Da Vinci to arbitrate their quarrel. The colorist and the designer made long addresses before the judge, each extolling himself and throwing contempt upon the other, and finally demanding that the case should be decided on the merits of their pictures. Mercury is sent to get them, but learns that they are dead and buried, and returns with a vast procession of ghostly pictures, which the assembled spirits criticise with sparkling wit. The shades of Socrates and Alexander wax angry and sarcastic at the anachronistic caricatures which had been made of them, until the judge arose in ire, and bestowed bitter reprimands upon the two painters, bidding them consider Raphael, who united nearly all the excellences of art by wise study of his great contemporaries. He then sentenced them to be bound in one yoke, to paint together for five centuries, and then perhaps gracious Jove would send them back to earth as one artist.

> "For thus the eternal Fates decree:
>   'One leg alone shall never run,
>   Nor two Half-Painters make but one.'"

"Eccentricity" is a didactic poem of four hundred and thirteen lines, portraying numerous ridiculous and affected characters such as are often met by the student of humanity, in ponderous and involved sentences which recall the profundities of Pope or Cowper. The following is the closing sentiment: —

> "O task sublime, to till the human soil,
>   Where fruits immortal crown the laborer's toil!
>   Where deathless flowers, in everlasting bloom,
>   May gales from heaven with odorous sweets perfume,
>   Whose fragrance still, when man's last work is done,
>   And hoary Time his final course has run,
>   Through ages back, with freshening power shall last,
>   Mark his long track, and linger where he passed!"

"The Paint-King" is a weird and mock-romantic poem of thirty-eight stanzas, describing the abduction of the fair Ellen by the Paint-King, who captivated her in the guise of a fascinating youth, with a mysterious picture of Pygmalion and Galatea. He swept her away through the air to a mountain-cave, and then appeared before her in his true aspect, with a face "like a palette of villanous dyes," sitting on a Titan's skull, and smoking a pipe twice as big as the Eddystone Lighthouse. He immersed her for seven days in a jug of oil, and then ground her up, spreading on his palette the blue of her eyes, the brown of her hair, the red of her lips, etc., to paint therewith the portrait of Geraldine the fairy. But he failed in the picture, which was to give him the fairy for a wife or to cost him his life, and Geraldine at once slew him and released Ellen from her pulverized state. As wild a fancy, surely, and as well wrought out, as any Hawthorne ever dreamed of.

Following "The Paint-King" were two poems, respectively "To a Lady, who Lamented that she had never been in Love," and "To a Lady who Spoke slightingly of Poets," — melodious stanzas, full of delicate sentiment and active fancy. Next came six sonnets, to West, Rembrandt, Tibaldi, the Luxembourg Gallery, and the magnificent tributes to the falling group in Angelo's 'Last Judgment' and Raphael's 'Three Angels before Abraham's Tent.' The London edition closed with four simple and touching ballads.

Allston sent a volume of his poems to Lady Beaumont, and Collins, who delivered it, wrote to him: "Southey said that, whatever defects some of them might have, he had no hesitation in saying that they could not have proceeded from any but a poetic mind; in which sentiment he was most cordially supported by Wordsworth, who was present at the time."

"Monaldi" is the title of an Italian romance which Allston composed in 1821 for publication in Richard H. Dana's serial of "The Idle Man." The sudden suspension of the periodical caused the author to throw his manuscript aside; but twenty years later he sought it out and gave it to the public. The story opens with an adventure in the Abruzzi Mountains, which leads the narrator to a secluded monastery wherein he discovers a weird and mysterious painting of Satan, on a golden throne, adored by an agonized mortal. This incident is described with a graphic vigor which confirms the author's renown as a teller of ghost-stories, and exemplifies how keenly he enjoyed the supernatural and how eagerly he received legendary and marvellous stories. These traits appear still more richly in such pictures as the Belshazzar and the Spalatro, the bandit-haunted forests, the sorceress of Endor. After its impressive beginning, the story is carried on with an easy grace and a revealing power which mark the author's masterly skill in construction, and his comprehension of the secret and terrible workings of love, jealousy, and revenge. In some parts the situations are appalling in their tragic power; but elsewhere there are bright and attractive passages on art and nature, in which the experience and reflections of the writer during his years of Roman life are vividly set forth. The heroine of the story is an ideally lovely creation, filled with spiritual life and strength, and recalling the lineaments of certain of the master's pictures. The hero is a painter, and his character is unfolded with great vigor and masterly analysis. The construction of the plot is faulty in parts, but the style is concise and simple, and often becomes eloquent and melodious. The book was translated into the German language.

Professor Felton thus criticises "Monaldi": "The style of this work is flowing, melodious, picturesque, and beautifully finished; many of its scenes are wrought up with a terrible power, more of them sparkle with all the graces of imagination and taste. There are paragraphs in that book in which the very soul of the author seems to pour itself out in strains of the richest melody; there are innumerable passages of such graphic beauty that no other hand could have traced them but his whose marvellous cunning painted for all coming time the Beatrice, Rosalie, and Amy Robsart."

Soon after 1830 Mr. Allston began the preparation of a series of lectures, which he was to have delivered before a select audience in Boston. He completed four of these lectures, and made the drafts of two others. They were edited by Richard H. Dana, Jr., and published at New York, in 1850, in a volume which also included Allston's poems. Professor Felton says that they "contain the essence of Allston's entire artistic life. . . . This is indeed a golden legacy to the art and literature of our country."

A note preliminary to the lectures carefully

defined the word *idea*, in the sense in which it should be used therein, as "the highest or most perfect *form* in which anything, whether of the physical, the intellectual, or the spiritual, may exist to the mind. There are two kinds of ideas, self-affirmed, and therefore not mere notions,— the *primary*, or manifestation of objective realities; and the *secondary*, or the reflex products of the mental constitution."

The "Introductory Discourse" opens with an exaltation of the mental pleasures, and proceeds to state and demonstrate the following proposition: "That the Pleasures in question have their true source in One Intuitive Universal Principle or living Power, and that the three Ideas of Beauty, Truth, and Holiness, which we assume to represent the *perfect* in the physical, intellectual, and moral worlds, are but the several realized phases of this sovereign principle, which we shall call *Harmony*." This is attended with a profound and philosophical analysis of the idea of Beauty, with its powers and limitations; a consideration of the imperishable pleasure of Truth, illustrated aptly in many ways; and a reverent contemplation of Goodness, and its resistless ultimate power. The divine harmony in which these principles are united is then proclaimed, and the manner and efficacy of the synthesis are set forth, — the argument ascending, as it were, in a continuous spiral, and at last resting above the stars.

The second lecture demonstrates that Art is distinguished from Nature by four great characteristics, namely, Originality; Human or Poetic Truth, the verifying principle by which the first is recognized; Invention, or the product of the Imagination, as grounded on the first and verified by the second; and Unity, the synthesis of all. There is a fine comparison, in the course of the argument, between Raphael and Ostade; and the power of Poetic Truth is demonstrated by glowing allusions to Shakespeare's Caliban, Sir Joshua Reynolds's Puck, the Farnese Hercules, and the Apollo Belvedere.

The third lecture was on the Human Form, and contains the following propositions: "First, that the notion of one or more standard Forms, which shall in all cases serve as exemplars, is essentially false, and of impracticable application for any true purpose of Art; secondly, that the only approach to Science, which the subject admits, is in a few general rules relating to Stature, and these, too, serving rather as convenient *expedients* than exact guides, inasmuch as, in most cases, they allow of indefinite variations; and, thirdly, that the only efficient Rule must be found in the artist's mind, — in those intuitive Powers which are above, and beyond, both the senses and the understanding; which, nevertheless, are so far from precluding knowledge, as, on the contrary, to require, as their effective condition, the widest intimacy with the things external, — without which their very existence must remain unknown to the artist himself." This thoughtful discourse closes with a brilliant comparison of Raphael and Michael Angelo, "the two great sovereigns of the two distinct empires of Truth, — the Actual and the Imaginative."

The fourth and last lecture treats of Composition in Art, which contains the following characteristics: "First, Unity of Purpose, as expressing the general sentiment or intention of the Artist. Secondly, Variety of Parts, as expressed in the diversity of shape, quantity, and line.

Thirdly, Continuity, as expressed by the connection of parts with each other, and their relation to the whole. Fourthly, Harmony of Parts." Variety is illustrated by Veronese's 'Marriage of Cana'; and the systems of lines of Claude and of Salvator Rosa are skilfully contrasted. Raphael, Tintoretto, Poussin, and Claude are considered in their early imitative idea; and Reynolds's defence of borrowing is reprehended.

The walls of Allston's studio were marked with over forty aphoristic sentences, which, as he told Mrs. Jameson, served as "texts for reflection before he began his day's work." He sometimes discussed their merits with visitors, and continually pondered them in his heart. From these articles of his artistic creed we select a half-dozen, almost at random, as expository of his character and genius.

"If an Artist love his Art for its own sake, he will delight in excellence wherever he meets it, as well in the works of another as his own. This is the test of a true love."

"The love of gain never made a Painter; but it has marred many."

"Distinction is the consequence, never the object, of a great mind."

"There is an essential meanness in the wish *to get the better* of any one. The only competition worthy of a wise man is with himself."

"Make no man your idol, for the best man must have faults; and his faults will insensibly become yours, in addition to your own. This is as true in Art as in morals."

"What *light* is in the natural world, such is *fame* in the intellectual; both requiring an *atmosphere* in order to become perceptible. Hence the fame of Michael Angelo is, to some minds, a nonentity; even as the sun itself would be invisible *in vacuo*."

As a word-painter Allston was almost as successful as in his own profession, and few richer pen-pictures can be found than those in which he describes the scenery of the Apennines, or a hot white summer noon in Rome, or the Alps at morning around Lake Maggiore. His conversation was no less brilliant than his writings, full of wisdom and sympathy and rich experience, and alike improving and inspiring to all who heard it. The colloquial accomplishment was not with him a lost art, and the humble home at Cambridgeport often heard marvellous discourses and reminiscences. The varied and picturesque experiences of an active lifetime in many lands were freely poured forth in accents of grace and vitality. One of his favorite themes was his sojourn in Rome, with the august memories of his friendship with Thorwaldsen, Coleridge, and Irving, and their rambles and discussions among the ruins and palaces of the Eternal City.

CHAPTER VIII.

Personal Traits. — System of Color. — Versatility. — Italianism. — Slight Influence on American Art.

Allston's personal appearance was such as would have distinguished him among a thousand. His figure was slender, but straight and active, and his air seemed serenely abstracted, when not enlivened by conversation. His broad and spiritual forehead was bordered by long white hair, which descended upon his shoulders in waving masses. His eyes appeared large and eloquent, and were somewhat projecting. His chin was short, but not receding. The general expression of the face indicated mildness and sweetness, bordering on effeminacy, yet there was that behind it which rendered it impossible for visitors to show undue familiarity or freedom. Mr. Allston's manner was so dignified and courtly that Collins, the Royal Academician, once said: "Were any one to meet Washington Allston in the street, with a sack of coals on his shoulders, he would at once recognize him as a gentleman."

John Howard Payne, in his later years, gave to Washington Irving the following laconic description of the master: "Allston was always the gentleman. Would talk by the hour. Liked to talk. A capital teller of ghost-stories. Would act them with voice, eyes, and gesture. Had touches of gentle humor. Rather indolent. Would lie late in bed. Smoked segars. A man of real genius. A noble painter. It was a pity he came back (in 1818); he would have risen to the head of his art, — been the greatest painter of his day." Charles Sumner also said: "Allston was a good man, with a soul refined by purity, exalted by religion, softened by love. In manner he was simple, yet courtly, — quiet, though anxious to please, — kindly to all alike, the poor and lowly not less than the rich and great. As he spoke, in that voice of gentlest utterance, all were charmed to listen ; and the airy-footed hours often tripped on far towards the gates of morning before his friends could break from his spell."

The delicate sensitiveness of the master was shown in many and peculiar ways. When india-rubber overshoes began to be worn, he purchased a pair, but could never put them on or remove them except with the tongs. He disliked the touch of metallic door-knobs, and usually interposed the skirt of his coat, or a handkerchief, between his hand and the metal.

One of the singular customs of the artist's household was that in relation to a fire on the hearth, which was kept up throughout the year, so that visitors were favored with the music of a few crackling brands, even during the sufficient heats of an August evening.

Allston was one of the most graceful dancers ever seen in Massachusetts, having been distinguished for a rare suppleness and ease. The cotillion was in high favor at that time, and happy was the lady who could secure him as a partner. He would sometimes find himself dancing almost alone, the others having ceased in order to observe and admire his unrivalled grace. This accomplishment was especially noticeable after Allston's first visit to Europe, while he was still young and delighted in society.

He was fond of reading metaphysical works, and had no less pleasure in wild and supernatural romances, tinged with *diablerie*. He perused "The Five Nights of St. Alban's" with a keen zest, and exulted in the works of Mrs. Radcliffe.

Jarves enumerates Allston's faults as "inequality of execution, imperfect modelling at times, not infrequent bad taste in details, and a forcible realism of feature and *pose* in some of his greatest figures, amounting almost to awkwardness and ugliness." In 1878 George Inness said that "Allston's misfortune was that the literary had too strong hold upon his mind, creating in him ideas which were grandiose."

Allston laid in his pictures in solid crude colors, and put them by for months, while the vehicle which he used hardened the pigments to a stony surface. When the long process of drying and hardening was over, he added tenderness and richness to their solidity and strength by the skilful application of transparent glazing colors. Some of his unfinished works still remain in their state of unrelieved hardness. He also experimented to a hazardous degree, and some of his works have already lost their subtlest qualities of transparency and brilliancy.

A recent critic (Miss Sarah Clarke) thus strikes the keynote of Allston's melodious system: "The method of this artist was to suppress all the coarser beauties which make up the substance of common pictures. He was the least *ad captandum* of workers. He avoided bright eyes, curls, and contours, glaring lights, strong contrasts, and colors too crude for harmony. He reduced his beauty to her elements, so that an inner beauty might play through her features. Like the Catholic discipline which pales the face of the novice with vigils, seclusion, and fasting, and thus makes room and clears the way for the movements of the spirit, so in these figures every vulgar grace is suppressed. No classic contours, no languishing attitudes, no asking for admiration, — but a severe and chaste restraint, a modest sweetness, a slumbering intellectual atmosphere, a graceful self-possession, eyes so sincere and pure that heaven's light shines through them, and, beyond all, a hovering spiritual life that makes each form a presence."

Ware attributes no small part of Allston's success to his general cultivation of mind, which enabled him to impart the vigor and elegance of learning to his designs, and to give his characters a notable dignity. Joined to this broad culture, and illuminating it, were the noble and elevated traits of the artist's soul, earnest truthfulness, unselfishness, simplicity, and consecration to the highest ends of art. It was impossible for a man who thus formed a conscience of his art either to make many pictures or much money. Another foundation of his fame was that he so often painted life-size figures, which gave him a correct and elevated manner of execution and a corresponding mental inspiration. Yet these works, though rivalling the great mediæval frescos in size, were finished with the conscientious exactness and minute finish of Dutch cabinet-pictures.

He advised a young artist studying in Europe: " Do not be satisfied with being one thing. The old masters did everything. They were sculptors and architects, as well as painters. Nay, they were poets and philosophers, as Michael Angelo and Leonardo da Vinci. They painted, also, all sorts of pictures, and succeeded in all. Titian, the best portrait, was also the best landscape, painter; at least, he was inferior only to Claude."

He could not endure the stilted allegorical compositions of the schools of West and Fuseli, and once said: "If you are going to paint a tub or a candlestick, paint a tub or a candlestick in very truth, and not an allegory therefor."

The versatility of Allston in painting at will historical compositions, portraits, ideal heads, landscapes, marines, and *genre* pictures was accompanied with a minute and delicate finish bestowed on all alike. It was matter of wonder, when his pictures were collected in Boston, how so much work could have been crowded into one short life, and that a crippled one. The grand figures of his prophets and kings were not more carefully and minutely painted than the accessories of still-life, — the vases, jewels, and backgrounds. But this versatility was fatal to the master's pre-eminence in American art, for life is not long enough for the noblest mind and deftest hand to attain illustrious excellence in so many departments of endeavor. He should have confined himself to small ideal subjects, with which he had full sympathy.

Allston's love for sublimity was hardly less than his devotion to beauty, though it was not so often displayed in his art. Not often in Nature affluent chiefly in beauty, did he seek sublimity, or attempt its delineation, but rather in the emotions of the human mind, remorse, woe, supernatural terror. In these themes he succeeded marvellously well, insomuch that his pictures leave an abiding and haunting impression in the mind. The sharp manifestations of passionate life are veiled in an atmosphere of divine glow and profound mystery, inviting the study of the most reflective and contemplative of men, and rich in simple genuineness and magnetic charm. Through this calm repose played the rhythmic melody of delicate repetitions of color, in the manner of Paul Veronese, forming what Allston himself called an echo of colors.

In expression, or the power of portraying emotions and dispositions, Allston found another of his noble characteristics, though he withheld a display of this gift in a majority of his pictures, preferring to paint calm and passionless faces, full of tender and thoughtful beauty, and giving free scope to the imagination. Dignity is paramount, a grand abstraction, a passive majesty. In his favorite domain of ideal female heads he rarely represented faces as beautiful in the popular acceptation, but as introspective, reposeful, silent, and inanimate. If beauty can exist without expression, it finds no more perfect exemplifications than Allston's 'Rosalie' and 'Beatrice,'— not even in Leonardo's 'Monna Lisa' nor Raphael's 'Fornarina.' This attribute of repose pervades almost all of the master's faces, and fills them with the spirit of contemplation and peace; and herein is the highest triumph of what Lord Napier of Merchiston called "the incomparable pencil of Allston."

Mr. Allston once said, "I never let a picture go out from my studio until I have finished it as well as I can"; and again (to Mrs. Jameson), "My industry should be measured, not by the pictures seen, but by those not seen." He took exception to Dunlap's declaration that he was indolent, saying, "I am famous among my acquaintances for industry: I paint every day: and never pass an hour without accomplishing something."

Every part of Allston's pictures was executed by his own hand, a fact which America has cause to mourn. Had he possessed such assistants as those of Raphael and other ancients to do the mechanical work, laying in the first colorings, and painting the unconsidered accessories, he might have adorned his country with hundreds of his noble conceptions, finished, in all essential parts, by his own hand. Under such supervision as he could have given, scores of young artists would have flocked to his side, relieving him of his day-laborer's drudgery and imbibing his spirit of grace and beauty, and the Cambridge studio would have been the birthplace of American art.

Tuckerman, one of the leading art-critics of America, thus characterizes Allston: "With the name of this great painter, painting reached its acme of excellence among us. In genius, character, life, and feeling, he emulated the Italian masters, partook of their spirit, and caught the mellow richness of their tints. Around his revered name cluster the most select and gratifying associations of native art; in each department he exhibited a mastery. . . . From an Alpine landscape, luminous with frosty atmosphere and sky-piercing mountains, to moonbeams flickering on a quiet stream, — from grand Scriptural to delicate fairy figures, — from rugged and solemn Jewish heads to the most ideal female conceptions, — from 'Jeremiah' to 'Beatrice,' and from 'Miriam' to 'Rosalie,' every phase of mellow and transparent, — almost magnetic color, graceful contours, deep expression, rich contrast of tints, — the mature, satisfying, versatile triumph of pictorial art, as we have known and loved it in the Old World, then and there, justified the name of American Titian, bestowed on Allston at Rome ; while the spiritual isolation and benignity, the instructive and almost inspired discourse, the lofty ideal, the religious earnestness, even the lithe frame, large, expressive eyes, and white flowing locks of Allston, his character, his life, conversation, presence, and memory, proclaimed the great artist."

Thirty-five years have passed since Allston's pencil fell from his weary hand, and American art has made noble progress. But whatever its achievements in those departments which are favored by modern taste, it has not yet surpassed — it has not equalled — the grandeur of the imaginative works of the great Carolinian. He strove for excellence, and loved it for its own sake, without thought of temporal considerations and emoluments, save as beautifully expressed in his own words: "Fame is the eternal shadow of excellence, from which it can never be separated."

Although a child of the New World and of the railway age, Allston's life and works, his face and manners, were those of another epoch, and partook of the dignity and power of the old masters of Italian art. And this was not because he had dwelt long amid the suggestive scenes of the classic lands, for his abode in Southern Europe was comparatively short in its duration, and occurred in the earlier part of his life. Powers became a dweller in Italy, yet never allowed his quaint Yankee traits to be obliterated; nor did Cole's long residence near the Apennines force him to forget the Catskills and the White Hills. Yet here, in one of the least prepossessing of New England villages we find an antique soul developing characteristics which would have been more congenial to the Greeks of the days of Pericles or the Romans of the sixteenth Christian century.

The dignity and lofty aims of true art were ever present in Allston's mind, and narrowed the compass of his achievements by increasing the conscientious demands which he made upon himself in the search after his exalted ideal. He was dissatisfied with his best works, however glorious they certainly were, because they came short of supreme excellence; and hence arose the frequent interruptions therein, as he laid down the pencil in hopeless humility. But although he was thus distrustful of his own abilities, his magnanimity disposed him to be an enlightened critic and a discriminating counsellor; and many were the artists who profited by his appreciative advice and sympathy, and hailed him as Master.

Allston should have spent his life in Italy, in the very presence of the works of his great guides in art. The British school exercised no influence upon his noble style, composed, as it was, of a strong originality mingled with the motives of the Italian leaders of the sixteenth century. His return to America was an abnegation of the wealth and distinction which awaited him abroad, but served to light a section of the home-land as from a high beacon. The atmosphere and the people were uncongenial to art, but its disciple stood fast amid the practicalities of the dullest era of American life, and lifted his rush-light in the darkness. Boston was indeed proud of him, and gave him generous orders;

but the melody of artistic inspiration had not yet thrilled through the air of the Puritan commonwealth, and Allston was bereft of adequate incitements.

And yet, when we consider the lofty genius of Allston, his rich transatlantic years, his peaceful and tranquil life, and the enthusiastic appreciation with which America received him, it is impossible to avoid a feeling that the master did not attain the best possible results. If he had devoted to his profession all the time which was wasted on dilettant diversions, and had avoided that colossal rock of offence, the 'Belshazzar's Feast,' he might have gathered about him the flower of American youth, and founded a new and noble school of Western art, prolific in illustrious works, and adding a Florentine or a Venetian elegance to the martial glories of the Republic. Herein he failed, through lack of victory-compelling effort, and left but as many pictures as could fill a large drawing-room; while American art still remains without a head, and becomes an appanage of Paris.

A LIST OF THE CHIEF PAINTINGS OF WASHINGTON ALLSTON, WITH THE NAMES OF THEIR PRESENT OWNERS.

⁎ *The names of the owners are in italics.*

⁎ *Some of the pictures herein noted are unfinished; and some are highly finished studies.*

UNITED STATES.

BOSTON. — *Museum of Fine Arts,* — Portrait of Mr. Harris; Elijah in the Desert, 1817; Portrait of Allston, 1805; Pilot-boat and Storm; copy of Paul Veronese's 'Marriage at Cana,' 1803; Landscape; The Prophetess; Una; Dido; Study of Lorenzo and Jessica; Female Head; The Troubadour; The Death of King John; Cupid; Sketch of Belshazzar's Feast; Sketch of Christ Healing the Sick. (Several of these are unfinished, and pertain to the Dana family. The new wing of the Museum, erected in 1878, contains the so-called Allston Room, devoted to these pictures, and to others by the same artist, loaned by their owners and by the Athenæum.) *Boston Athenæum,* — Belshazzar's Feast; Landscape; Isaac of York; Polish Jew; The Student; The Opening of the Casket, 1802; Portrait of Benjamin West, 1814. *Mrs. George M. Barnard, Jr.,* — Landscape. *Nathan Appleton,* — Rosalie. *Mrs. George Ticknor,* — The Valentine. *Mrs. Stephen H. Bullard,* — Beatrice. *Richard Sullivan,* — A Lady. *Miss E. Jackson,* — Lorenzo and Jessica. *William Gray,* — The Sisters. *John A. Lowell,* — Amy Robsart. *Dr. Thomas Dwight,* — A Polish Jew. *H. W. Foote,* — Italian Landscape. *Miss Pratt,* — Landscape. *Mrs. John Codman*, — Pilot-boat in a Storm. *Frederick R. Sears*, — Tuscan Girl; Miriam. *Mrs. George R. Baldwin*, — Polyphemus. *Richard H. Dana, Jr.*, — Ideal female figure. *Richard H. Dana*, — Sketch for Belshazzar's Feast, 1817; Sketch for Christ Healing the Sick, 1817; Portrait of S. T. Coleridge (unfinished), 1805; Portrait of Allston (unfinished), 1805; Landscape; Head of Jeremiah; Titania's Court. *Mrs. S. Hooper*, — The Evening Hymn; Swiss Landscape. *Mrs. Paine*, — The Young Troubadour. *Dr. Bigelow*, — Landscape. *Mrs. Benjamin Greene*, — Head of a Jew. *Rev. J. F. W. Ware*, — A Child's Portrait. *W. H. Gardiner*, — The Witch of Endor.

MILTON. — *Mrs. M. E. Eustis*, — Mrs. Allston; William Ellery Channing. DORCHESTER. — *Mrs. Robert C. Hooper*, — Italian Shepherd Boy. BROOKLINE. — *Ignatius Sargent*, — Poor Author and Rich Publisher. *Mrs. W. C. Cabot*, — Landscape. *Mrs. J. E. Cabot*, — Roman Lady. *Mrs. Judge Wells* (Longwood), — The Indian Summer. *James M. Codman*, — Landscape. CAMBRIDGE. — *Prof. C. E. Norton*, — David Playing the Harp before Saul, 1805; The Romans and the Serpent of Epidaurus, 1805. *Mrs. Gurney*, — The Mother and Child, 1814. *Allston Heirs*, — Jason (an immense unfinished work). MEDFORD. — *E. T. Hastings*, — Una (unfinished). WORCESTER. — *Massachusetts Insane Asylum*, — The Angel Delivering St. Peter from Prison, 1812.

NEW HAVEN. — *Yale College Art-Gallery*, — Jeremiah. PROVIDENCE. — *W. F. Channing*, — Portrait of Francis Channing. NEWPORT. — *Redwood Library*, — Portrait of

Robert Rogers. WASHINGTON, D. C. — *George Bancroft*, — Head of St. Peter. PHILADELPHIA, PA. — *Academy of Fine Arts*, — The Dead Man Revived by Elisha's Bones. *Mrs. General Barstow*, — Bandits (Donna Mencia?). NEW YORK CITY. — *George Sherman*, — A Landscape. *William J. Flagg*, — Moonlight Landscape. FISHKILL-ON-HUDSON. — *Mrs. Headley*, — Portrait of Mrs. William Channing. SCHENECTADY. — *Rev. Dr. Robert Lowell*, — Landscape. CHARLESTON, S. C. — *Misses Allston*, — A Landscape; Portrait of Allston's Mother.

ENGLAND.

LONDON. — *British National Portrait Gallery*, — Portrait of Mr. S T. Coleridge. *British Museum*, — Several sketches. *Stafford House*, — The Angel Uriel Standing in the Sun. PETWORTH. — Jacob's Dream; Contemplation; The Repose in Egypt; two cabinet pictures. CAMBRIDGE. — *Jesus College*, — Portrait of Coleridge.

MISSING.

Nine pictures painted before going abroad. — Portrait of Mr. King; Cardinal Bentivoglio (copy); young Mr. Waterhouse; W. E. Channing; three other Channing portraits; Head of Judas Iscariot; St. Peter.

Twenty-six pictures painted in Europe. — French Soldier; Rocky Coast; Landscape with Horsemen; The Poet's Ordinary; Landscape; Cupid and Psyche; Diana; Dr. King; Robert Southey; three ideal pictures at Bristol; Mrs. King; Rebecca at the Well; Morning in Italy; Donna Mencia; Clytie; Hermia and Helena; Falstaff; Samuel Williams; Mediterranean Coast.

Pictures painted after 1818. — Florimel; The Massacre of the Innocents; Gabriel Setting the Guard of the Heavenly Host; The Spanish Girl; Edwin; Falstaff.

Several others have been destroyed by fire, and others disappeared during the great Civil War.

INDEX.

Abernethy, 83.
Albro's Eulogy, 154.
Allston Family, The, 7, 97.
Allston quoted, 11, 16, 19, 28, 31, 35, 36, 37, 39, 41, 42, 45, 48, 54, 58, 62, 69, 70, 74, 90, 92, 95, 96, 102, 110, 114, 117, 119, 120, 121, 122, 124, 131, 137, 141, 149, 151, 158, 159, 161, 166-70, 177, 180, 182.
American Scenery, 115.
American Titian, The, 50, 72.
Amy Robsart, 113.
Angel Delivering St. Peter, The, 61.
Angel Uriel, The, 81.
Angelo, Michael, 42, 46.
Antislavery, 96.
Artistic Raptures, 37, 41.
Authorship, 156.

Banditti, 29.
Beatrice, 111.
Beaumont, Sir George, 61.
Belshazzar's Feast, 119, 146, 83.
Bentivoglio's Portrait, 19.
Boston Harbor, 92.
Boston in 1818, 93.
Boston Studios, 54, 93.

Caffé Greco, 43.
Cambridgeport, 131.
Carolina, Parting from, 27.
Channing, Dr. W. E., 18, 23, 52, 76, 98.
Chantry, 96.
Charleston, 25.
Childhood, 11.
Churchman, Allston a, 78, 134.
Clarke, Miss S., 141, 138, 175.
Classmates, 24.

Coleridge, S. T., 49, 62, 66, 73, 75, 78, 86, 98.
College-life, 15.
Collins, William, 60, 80, 95, 101, 163, 172.
Conversation, 170.
Crawford, the Sculptor, 140.

Dana, Chief Justice, 24, 108.
Dana, Richard H., 18, 149.
Dancing, 174.
Dead Man Revived, The, 69.
Death of Allston, 152.
Death of Mrs. Allston, 76.
Death of King John, 113.
Dear Old England, 90.
Decline, 149.
Designs Engraved, 117.
De Veaux, 101.
Dickens, Charles, 146.

Early Drawings, 16.
Elijah in the Desert, 105.
Evening Hymn, The, 113.
Exhibition of 1839, 142.

Fascination, 44.
Felton, Professor, 147, 165.
Flagg, G. W., 102.
Flagg, J. B., 104.
Flaxman, 83.
Florence, 40.
Florimel, 111.
Fraser, Charles, 25, 115.
Fuller, Margaret, 141, 143.
Fuseli, Henry, 32, 34.

Ghost-stories, 75, 79.
Government Commissions, 139.
Grave of Allston, The, 155.

INDEX.

Greenough, Horatio, 99, 140, 146.
Grief, 77.

Harding, Chester, 94, 123, 140, 144.
Harvard in 1796, 22.
Haydon, Benjamin R., 62.
Healy, G. P. A., 140.
Hogarthean Humor, 36.
Homesickness, 92.
Humboldts, The, 43.

Industry, 180.
Innocence, 79, 81.
Irving, Washington, 44, 53, 79, 81, 88, 102.
Ishes, The, 144.
Italian Landscape, 115.
Italy's Influence, 38, 135.
Jacob's Dream, 84, 88.
Jameson, Mrs., 118, 137.
Jeremiah, 107.

Lamb, Charles, 86.
Lawrence, Sir Thomas, 91.
Lectures on Art, 165.
Leslie, Charles R., 56-7, 59.
Liverpool, 55.
London, 33, 55.
Longfellow, Henry W., 75, 145-7.
Lorenzo and Jessica, 114.
Lowell's Pen-sketch, 131.

Madonna, A Modern, 70.
Malbone, 16, 20, 25, 31.
Marion's Cavalry, 9.
Marriage, 52, 108.
Martin, John, 71, 122.
Miriam, 112.
Mistake, The Great, 54, 88, 184.
Modelling, 49, 72.
Monaldi, 163.
Morning Years, 28.
Morse, Professor S. F. B., 53, 63, 77, 97, 138, 139, 153.

Napoleon's Trophies, 36.
Newport, 13.
Nobility, The British, 82.
Northcote, the Painter, 35.

Paint-King, The, 161.
Paris, Visits to, 36, 80.
Payne, John Howard, 63, 77, 173.
Percival, James Gates, 100.
Personal Appearance, 45, 131, 147, 148, 172.

Petworth, 85.
Physical Troubles, 65, 87.
Poetry, 25, 52, 68, 75, 110, 114, 156.
Portrait, 51.
Prescott, William H., 119, 145.

Raphael, 41.
Religion, 134, 152.
Reynolds, Sir Joshua, 32, 35.
Robinson, H. Crabbe, 86.
Roman Lady, 113.
Rome, 40.
Rosalie, 110.
Royal Academy, The, 31, 35, 95.

Sickness in England, 66.
Sisters, The, 114.
Southey, 67, 68, 74, 163.
Spalatro's Vision, 116, 104.
Spanish Girl, The, 112.
Staigg, Richard M., 105.
Stuart, Gilbert, 98, 121.
Studios, 93, 132.
Sully, Thomas, 98, 101, 121.
Sumner, Charles, 38, 75, 114, 122, 145, 146, 155, 173.
Swiss Landscape, 115.
Switzerland, 39.
Sylphs of the Seasons, 68, 157.

Thorwaldsen, 43.
Ticknor, George, 140, 145.
Titianesque Color, 50.
Trumbull, John, 60.
Tuckerman, H. T., 142, 181.
Turner, J. M. W., 39, 85.
Tuscan Girl, The, 114.
Two Painters, The, 159.

Valentine, The, 109.
Vanderlyn, 36, 40.
Venetian Coloring, 37, 50, 57.
Veronese, Paul, 37, 57.

Waccamaw, 7, 9, 26.
Waterhouse. Dr., 23.
Waterston, Rev. Dr., 22, 146, 148.
Weir, of West Point, 50, 148.
West, Benjamin, 31, 33, 54, 56, 65, 71.
Willis, N, P., 140.
Wordsworth, William, 62, 73, 140, 145, 163.